The Long March
to Paris

The Long March
to Paris

Reminiscences of a Dane in Prussian Service
Throughout the Napoleonic Era to the Fall of
the French Capital and Emperor, 1814

Henrik Steffens

LEONAUR

The Long March to Paris
Reminiscences of a Dane in Prussian Service
Throughout the Napoleonic Era to the Fall of
the French Capital and Emperor, 1814
by Henrik Steffens

First published under the title
Adventures on the Road to Paris During the Campaigns of 1813-14

Leonaur is an imprint of Oakpast Ltd

Copyright in this form © 2010 Oakpast Ltd

ISBN: 978-0-85706-403-5 (hardcover)
ISBN: 978-0-85706-404-2 (softcover)

http://www.leonaur.com

Contents

Translator's Preface

The wish to place within the reach of English readers some interesting remarks on the state of political feeling in Germany at the time of Napoleon's occupation of the country, as well as some graphic details of the war of liberation, has been the chief inducement to select the following passages from the life of Henry Steffens. The short personal narrative which precedes the sketches of the war can hardly be called an abridged translation. The substance is culled from six or seven volumes written in the peculiarly rambling style of German autobiographers, and it is rather a selection of the salient points in the author's picture of his character and history connected by some slight touches given in the hope of so introducing the autobiographer to the acquaintance of the readers, that they may accompany him with kinder sympathy through the events of the campaigns.

The *Memoirs of Henry Steffens* (*Was ich erlebte*) were published in Breslau in 1841, in ten volumes *octavo*. They are continued up to the year 1840, at which time he wrote from Berlin—"I am now, through the gracious favour of the King, the kindness of men in power, and the friendship of many distinguished men, able in peaceful happiness to devote the last years of my life to science." In 1845 Schelling concluded a public address at Berlin in honour of the memory of Steffens in the following words:—"And if we have watched with sorrow the failure of his bodily strength, we have also rejoiced to see the mind still firm in power to the last; and those who in his later years have heard the full outpouring of his rich discourse on the highest themes, while his soul glowed with heart-winning benevolence, will join with me in saying that he died in his youth at last."

Chapter 1

Family Records

In the year '90 of the last century, (1790), my youngest brother was an ensign quartered in the fortress of Rendsburg. The officers of the garrison were not in point of cultivation even favourable specimens of an army which in the course of a seventy years' peace had fallen into stupid inactivity, and my brother, who sought to keep pace with the intellectual development of that exciting period, was glad to form an intimacy with a young French officer, an emigrant of high birth, whose society at least afforded him an opportunity of improvement in the French language. It was common with the emigrants at that time to anticipate their restoration with the utmost confidence; this young man, therefore, discoursed incessantly on the grandeur and riches of his family, and as he knew my brother's slender means, he was lavish in his promises of future favour, regarding him as a highly-educated young officer, who might one day be worthy of patronage in France.

Though my brother neither cared for his friend's promises nor shared his hopes, he listened with good nature to the boasting history of a long line of noble ancestors, and when asked to give in return some records of his own descent, which the young exile presumed must have been noble, though less illustrious than his own, he promised to comply. After some delay he produced a tin case which contained an ancient document. It was a parchment deed; at the foot was a blue silk ribbon worked in silver, to which a box containing a huge seal was fixed. "Here is my patent of nobility," said my brother, and the Frenchman acknowledged with chagrin that not one of the records of his noble family looked half so splendid. After studying it for some days he returned it, lamenting that his small skill in the German language was not sufficient to decipher it: he begged for a translation, and my brother indulged him with the following:—

Be it made known to all by these presents, that we the Elders of the Worshipful Guild of Surgeons and Barbers of the town of Wilster in the duchy of Holstein, certify that the worthy and highly-skilled master Nicholas Zimmermann hath appeared before us in behalf of Henry Steffens, the lawfully-born son of the honourable and worthy Henry Steffens, citizen and brandy-distiller, and maketh oath that the aforesaid Henry Steffens hath fulfilled his three years' apprenticeship to the said Nicholas Zimmermann, and hath conducted himself towards his master and all persons as a decent, industrious, and honourable student, (and so forth).

"A noble family indeed!" exclaimed the scornful emigrant. It is scarcely necessary to add that the intimacy ended with the disclosure. I still possess this document, which is the only family record in existence. It is natural for every man to uphold the honour of his ancestry: while therefore I confess that my grandfather's calling was not precisely that which I should most desire to be able to record, I must be allowed to urge that the pernicious article he manufactured had not been in those days so destructively abused as it has in later times. I therefore persist in honouring his memory as a worthy burgher of the town of Wilster. His life besides had begun under better prospects: my great-grandfather had been a rich merchant, and had failed; my father, though born after his death, used to repeat family legends of the large baskets full of silver plate which were carried from the house on his misfortunes.

My grandfather, the only child of the once rich merchant, took refuge with some distant relatives in Surinam; he married a Dutch woman, and he returned to his own country before he had realized an independent fortune.

My father was born in Berbice in 1744; being of an enterprising character, it was not surprising that he chose surgery for his profession, since industry and talent so applied were sure to obtain a position of high respectability. He accompanied the Danish troops as an army surgeon to Mecklenburg, when that war with Russia was impending which had it been declared must have ended so disastrously for Denmark. When peace was ratified without a conflict my father went to Copenhagen to complete his studies; on them he expended all his small resources: that they were not confined to the mere subjects of his profession was evident by his intimate acquaintance with literature in general, whether poetry, natural history, or what was then called philosophy. He was a man of strong understanding and acute feeling, and when he was sent as surgeon of the district to Odsherred, a remote but highly productive country of north-east Siaelland, he had the good fortune to win the heart of the daughter of a considerable landed proprietor named Bang, a member of one of the first families in the country.

A few years after his marriage my father was appointed to superintend the establishment of an hospital at Stavanger, on the coast of Norway, and I, his second son, was born there a few months after his arrival. He was stationed a few years subsequently in Trondheim as regimental surgeon, and afterwards returned to Denmark, and in the same capacity was stationed in Helsingör, in Roeskilde, and then in Copenhagen, where my mother died; lastly he removed to Rendsburg, where he died himself.

We were six in family, four sons and two daughters. It has been our fate to be scattered from our youth, and I think with sadness of the few who yet remain, and of the far separated graves of the departed, while I, the only survivor of the brothers, am finishing my days in a country of adoption, having reached an age exceeding that of my brothers or my father. My three brothers all were distinguished in their professions, and obtained the notice of their sovereign.

I was born in 1773; three weeks later my friend Ludwig Tieck was born in Berlin, and the same day Hardenberg (Novalis) was born at Wiessenfels.

One of my earliest recollections is of the journey across Norway in the depth of winter, when I accompanied my parents from Trondheim to Helsingör in December, 1779. I travelled in a sledge with an apothecary named Bull, grandfather of the celebrated violinist. Closely packed up as we were, I was conscious of little besides the frequent upsetting of the sledge. Once, in particular, I found myself lying in the snow in the dark; I must have been sleeping, and was awakened by the concussion, and heard the exclamation "The fifth time!"

I have since often heard how nearly it had been our last: we were travelling through Drivdalen, a deep valley of the high Dovre pass; the road ran by the side of an abyss, a river foamed beneath; the road leaned towards the precipice on one side, while a high wall of rock rose abruptly on the other; just there our sledge was overturned, and had we not fallen against some props of a rotten railing, there would have been little now to tell either of Ole Bull or me.

I have a vivid impression of our first residence in Helsingör. A small street led to the Sound. Ours was the last house on the strand, and a high flight of steps led to the first floor. My parents took possession of the desolate-looking, empty rooms under many hardships; a little furniture was gradually collected and arranged, but the winter passed heavily away in the midst of family anxieties; there seemed little prospect of any practice for my father in his profession, and household cares and wants were pressing. I remember sad, gloomy days when my father became impatient and morose, and my mother moved quietly about in silent gentle sorrow: it was then that my whole soul first cling to her in love.

We were sent to a day-school. I was a precocious child; I had been able to read very early, and soon began to attempt little compositions both in prose and verse, but it was not then the custom to notice and encourage any unusual attainments in children. My father was a man of strong impulse. Endless annoyances consequent on his narrow circumstances had made him sterner than was natural to his really kind disposition: he was besides an admirer of Rousseau; we children therefore gained but little sympathy from him for many hardships which we suffered, and much unfair treatment which we underwent at school. My mother grieved for us, and longed to temper the severity with which we were brought up; but her drooping health kept her from active interference, and she was accustomed to yield in all things to her husband. Our lot would have been harder still had not his genuine love for her often restrained and softened him.

I must record the first very deep grief which wrung my childish feelings. We had a dog, older than myself, who was as much a member of the family as any of the children, or as the faithful maid, Maren, who lived with us from my father's marriage till his death. He became so diseased that it was thought impossible to keep him; my father determined that he should be drowned, but would not let a stranger do the work. I fancy yet I see how the dear animal followed my father with a loving look and sprang into the boat with signs of joy, for he had been accustomed to go with him in all his journeys—how the mother, the children, and the maid remained behind in sad suspense—how, clinging round our sick mother, we all felt united and endeared to each other by a common sorrow—and how, when we had waited long in speechless expectation, our father appeared again in tears, and we all sobbed aloud—it was the first grief which we all understood and shared together.

My father's new house was very different. There was a long row of windows on the ground-floor, and a gable story above: it was of wood, but gaily painted, and the cheerful, richly furnished rooms might be seen through the bright windows; a large reception-room extended the whole length of the *façade* behind, which was adorned by chandeliers, and was kept closed excepting when large parties were received. That was my father's season of prosperity: he had obtained the largest practice in the wealthy town; he was able to indulge his taste for society, and all the principal inhabitants assembled often in his hospitable house.

We were allowed to observe those great assemblies only from a distance, for it was then not customary to introduce children in society: we used to stand in the court behind the house, and peep with eager curiosity into the brilliantly lighted room; we could see the card-tables and observe the company as they moved about and talked, and my imagination used to be filled with a fantastic notion of the wonderful importance of the things they must be saying.

There was no spot, however, in our whole grand house, so bright and happy as the cheerful children's room; that was a charming scene of true enjoyment: beyond the court we saw our neat pretty garden, which stretched out to the Sound, and before us lay the Sound itself, crowded often by many hundred ships of every nation.

1785.—In my twelfth year my father was obliged, as regimental surgeon, to remove to Roeskilde. Few have taken such intense delight in all that is beautiful and wonderful in nature as I have throughout life. The country near Roeskilde is very lovely: the town stands in the deepest recess of a bay of the Cattegat, which sweeps far into the land; the waters were once deep enough for vessels of large size to approach the town, but the bay has become shallow, and none but very small craft are able now to float. The shores all round are richly wooded, and we used to count from our garden no less than eighteen churches, scattered over the bright landscape.

The pastoral tranquillity of the scene was most attractive to young minds, accustomed to a bold coast and a roaring sea, and it was there, roving in quiet, contemplative enjoyment, that my love of natural philosophy began; I collected plants, and, assisted by an old folio borrowed from my father's library, learnt to examine and arrange them under their barbarous Latin names; but Kruger's *Natural Philosophy* was my greatest treasure. I remember the industry with which I studied Newton's theory till I found that without some degree of mathematical knowledge the attempt was hopeless; our school taught no mathematics, and I searched in vain for works upon the subject in my father's library, but I did not rest till I obtained one, and then I soon was competent to follow Kruger's meaning.

I owe all my religious impressions to my mother; truly I may call her the guardian angel of my life; she was so in the most solemn sense of the expression, and when, in later years, in the midst of confusion and distraction, I have felt the warnings of reproving conscience, her anxious, thoughtful look has risen in my memory, the same as when in childhood she first taught me to know and love something beyond this world. She lived continually in the expectation of approaching death, and I remember regarding her as a sanctified being, belonging to the world where she was going rather than to that on which I in my young years was entering.

Once, when she was supposed to be dying, the secluded sanctuary of the sick room, which had been closed to us for weeks, was opened to the children: we all stood round the bed; my father was bent down, overpowered; I was to read the prayer. My mother raised herself; and how shall I describe the comfort when her sweet voice spoke of her joy and thankfulness, and of the faith with which she left us in the hands of God? I remember falling on my knees and wishing that I might die too with my mother.

But what shall I say of the hours which I passed in her sick room when she recovered from that dangerous crisis—of that closer intercourse which I enjoyed with her, and which lasted till her death? They were not times of prayer, nor yet of teaching—something of both: her gentle encouragement gave me power to speak; I imparted every newly acquired light, every idea, every doubt. I never remember her spirits to have been either excited or depressed—all was placid and resigned; and even when she spoke of her relation to my father, which, in a religious point of view, did not fulfil her earnest longings, it was always in a tender and forbearing tone.

My parents' prosperous circumstances darkened when they quitted Helsingör. They then feared, and the event proved how justly, that the rural district would afford no compensation for the ample income they were obliged to leave. After a time my father, finding that his pay alone could not support the most frugal household, begged to be exchanged into an infantry regiment stationed in Copenhagen; we therefore abandoned our small but pleasant home in Roeskilde, with hopeful expectation of finding better fortune in the capital: such hopes are often disappointed, and they were so in my parents' case; yet it was long before they were quite abandoned, and in the mean time the children at least were happy.

The multiplicity of new objects in the capital excited my imagination and bewildered my intellect in a strange degree: the quiet harmony of mind which I had enjoyed in our retreat at Roeskilde had deserted me, never, alas! to return in such perfection. I was, for a time, thrown much on my own resources, and I perceived with dismay that facts escaped me, and knowledge of the most elementary character became confused, and that my mind was tending towards a sort of chaos—happily that chaos proved the teeming precursor of another state of order, but it was not surprising that while I was in that condition, a young man who was engaged to direct our studies previously to our examination for admission into the university, should pronounce me utterly incapable of ever realizing any extent of knowledge.

My father had hoped much from my abilities, and dismissed the tutor, whom he blamed for want of competence. I cannot say much of the attainments of his successor, but his anxiety to do his utmost for us was extreme; and I had used the short interval between the attendance of the two instructors with such determined diligence, that when the day of examination arrived I passed, as well as my brothers, with considerable credit,

On my mother's side we had many relations in Copenhagen, who were rich and filled important stations. My mother's brother held an office the title of which I cannot exactly remember, but it was one of the highest in the state, and he called himself De Bang; we paid him a ceremonious visit, and were each presented in our turn. I have a chilling recollection of his stiff grandeur, and of the proud civility of the wife, who scarcely condescended to be called aunt. These were the people whom we had thought so much about when we were at a distance; there was a strange contrast between our satisfaction in the relationship when we were far off, and our mortification when we approached them—then we were honoured, now oppressed, by the connection; we may have judged too harshly the feelings which prompted our cold reception, but the inevitable result was to exasperate my father's proud spirit and increase the independence of his temper.

Our relationship to another uncle, Professor Bang, was far differently acknowledged; he was a man of true benevolence, though narrow in his views on many subjects, especially religion. As a physician, enjoying the confidence of the most distinguished persons in the country, he had many opportunities of indulging in works of charity, and he was ever ready to do good service to every member of his family. I never call to mind the diminutive figure, and the round face beaming with good humour and benevolence, without remembering with gratitude all the unwearied pains he took for my advancement, and without feeling deep regret that, for his sake alone, I have not more fulfilled his generous hopes.

I am still highly entertained when I remember the incidents of my first romance; it occurred when I was hardly fifteen; my enthusiasm for the beautiful in nature, with the habit of seeing all things through an atmosphere of poetry, was sure to lead me to invest some living object with my dreamy notions of perfection. There was a girls' school opposite our house; my divinity was soon selected, and it is impossible to say how much of her ideal charms owed their existence to the closed blinds, through which alone I had an opportunity of worshipping across the street.

A passion could not exist without a confidant; to fill the aching void, I chose a schoolfellow, whom we had left behind at Roeskilde, and a secret correspondence with him, filled with my glowing effusions, completed all my wishes.

One of the strict rules in our family forbade that any letters should be sent without being first read over to my father. I tried to hint my important communication in mysterious language, and to involve the sentences so that the meaning might escape detection; and my hopes to that effect were stronger, as my brothers had also letters to be read, and my father often took but little notice of them.

My turn came—my heart beat violently; my father had scarcely seemed to hear my brothers; but I had only just begun when he laid down his pen and listened with intense attention. I read with trembling voice, and tried to skip the subject, but it went on through the whole epistle—"What stuff have you got hold of?" he exclaimed in cool displeasure, and he took my letter from me. Such a scene of dismay succeeded! My brothers were terrified. "Leave the room," said my father; and as I went I saw my poor mother lift herself up from the couch in amazement and dismay.

An hour passed while my brothers crowded round to know my sin, and I stood a silent culprit. The old maid-servant came in—"Oh, master Henry! how could you grieve your poor sick mother so?" The tutor was sent for; and in the very depth of my despair I almost laughed when I overheard him say, "Such a letter! and the boy not even confirmed yet!" I was recalled to the paternal presence; my father had taken up the affair in a most serious light—what could I wish more? I now was a miserable lover, persecuted by my parents! My romance could not be more perfect; it was a humiliating descent when truth obliged me to confess that a distant look through the school window-blinds was all I had on which to build it. I was annihilated with jokes and ridicule; but my young spirits soon rose again, and helped me to take a whimsical view of the affair, and so to stand as conqueror on the ruins of my first attachment.

I have since learned that my parents were, in fact, highly I amused, though they thought it right to seem severe; and that they were delighted with evidences of power in my composition, which led them to expect great things from my opening talent. I must also confess that when the letter, some years afterwards, came into my hands, I found, to my surprise, touches of genuine poetry, and such boldness in the images and vigour of expression as I have never equalled in any later compositions.

My mother died, or rather faded gradually away; gently and progressively as her end approached, her death came at last as a terrible surprise upon us—so little did there seem to warn us of the final change. My whole existence seemed to hang upon her last faint breath. Every one of those long-past hours when my soul used to join with hers in pure devotion swept at that instant through my memory, and conscience whispered, for the first time, that other feelings and new hopes had sprung up to estrange me from that holy intercourse, and I felt a trembling dread that I had parted from the sanctuary for ever The minister passed us as he left her room; he seemed greatly affected, and we were told to enter. We surrounded the bed.

Our mother lay with placid look, apparently without suffering; she raised herself and blessed us; the picture of her glorified countenance—radiant with an expression we had never seen before—her large lustrous eye, and her cheek flushed with a passing tint of rose, is still before me; her usually low voice sounded clearer than we were used to hear it when she turned to me, and said, "Henry! you must preach the Gospel of your Lord. He has chosen you and bestowed gifts upon you for his service; be true to him and to yourself, and may God bless you." She sank back, her eyes closed, and we were taken away; a few minutes later, and the door stood open; we looked on the departed, and I knelt in an agony of tears beside the bed; all that my talents or my tastes had led me to desire, all my bright hopes and prospects were offered up at that moment. I vowed solemnly to accomplish my mother's wish; I resolved that henceforth I must be devoted to the ministry.

Alas for human nature! life in full vigour will vindicate its right; but that sad hour has borne a keen reproof when I have thought of the solemn vow, and how it has never been fulfilled. It is true, I felt convinced that my mother erred in her judgment of my character, and in her belief that I had an especial calling for the sacred office; yet not the less did her dying words lie heavily upon my conscience. In the midst of intellectual delights and in the most successful studies, I have felt that, after all, the clearest truth which I could realize was the darkness of her grave; I know no truer evidence of life than her death; and if, oppressed by cares or bewildered in the intricate mazes of obscure philosophy, I have preserved the seed of true religion, however far too little cherished or improved—if I have kept that seed deep in my heart, and have not dared to make a light or vain display of it upon my lips—for this I have to bless that death-bed scene, which has been a holy treasure through my life. I must not omit to describe a most important epoch of my life.

It was the time when the history of the modern world was to begin afresh—when all Europe, even all mankind, in some degree suffered a convulsion— it was the time of the Revolution.

I was sixteen. My father came home in great excitement; he called all his sons about him; we gazed with wonder at his agitation, and waited anxiously to learn his news. "Children!" said he, "you are to be envied; what a period of happiness and prosperity now lies before you! and if you do not now work out your independence, the fault will be your own; all crushing distinctions of rank are at an end—all poverty will disappear—and small and great will all be armed alike, to fight the same battle, on the same field. Oh that I were young like you! but my powers have been crippled; barriers have restrained me, which will not be opposed to you."

His emotion was so great that he burst into tears, and it was long before he could proceed. We had lived in such seclusion that we knew little of the movements in Paris, which had given warning of the crisis. My father at length told us of the first scenes in the Palais Royal— of the enthusiasm of the people—of their resistance to the reigning power—of the hopes that they would succeed;—and lastly, of the storming of the Bastile, and the liberation of the victims of despotic power.

It was a wonderful time; the Revolution was not French, but European—not so much of governments as of sentiments and opinions; it took deep root in millions of hearts; a sentence had gone forth against mouldering institutions, a victory was won over useless, humiliating distinctions, and the revolution was complete even where no open effort had been made. I was inspired with a boundless hope, and fancied that my whole future was transplanted into a new and richer soil.

CHAPTER 2

Departure From Copenhagen

The hopes which had induced my father to reside in Copenhagen had not been fulfilled, and his circumstances became more and more oppressive. At length, under the idea that he might meet with more success in his profession, or at least live more happily in Holstein, his native province, he obtained permission to exchange into a regiment that was quartered in Rendsburg. My brothers were already fixed in their professions, and when my father quitted Copenhagen I left it also to become a tutor to three young children in the family of a near relation at Odsherred.

I was eighteen, and no way qualified for the duties which I was obliged to undertake. I was taken from the university while my most important course of study was just beginning; my regret and mortification were extreme, and they deprived me of the power to enjoy the long-wished for freedom of a country-life and all the objects in nature which were to me so peculiarly attractive. I would gladly forget a period which I feel was destitute of good both to my pupils and myself, and which was terminated unexpectedly by the second of two accidents which befell me.

I had heated and tired myself one day on a botanizing excursion, and had entered a farmhouse to ask for a glass of brandy. The use of brandy on all occasions was then a general custom. I had scarcely emptied the glass when the woman started, and told me in an agony of distress that she had given me by mistake brandy containing arsenic. My terror was extreme: I used such remedies as were at hand, but suffered dreadfully. After some time I was put, half dead, into a carriage and taken back to Odsherred, where I lay for many days in a dangerous condition. My recovery was, however, complete, and I have since felt no ill effects from the accident.

My second casualty was followed by more lasting consequences. I fell asleep one very hot day in an open field; my hat fell off and left my head exposed to the full power of a burning sun. How long I had remained I cannot tell when a countryman found me lying in a state of insensibility. I recovered partly on being taken home, but my head was seriously affected. The relation in whose house I lived had no doubt observed how little I was qualified to perform the office of a teacher, and was glad to seize the opportunity to replace me by one more efficient; he therefore removed me immediately to Copenhagen and placed me in the hospital where my Uncle Bang attended.

The hospital for the sick in Copenhagen is arranged to admit patients of all classes in society, and the ward in which I was placed was appropriated to the use of students at the university and young men of respectable families. I was nearly convalescent when an incident occurred which excited my deepest interest. A young student occupied a bed opposite tome; he was in the last stage of consumption, frightfully emaciated, and unable to speak except by a most painful effort. Yet he did not seem to suffer nor to be aware of his approaching end: his whole thoughts were occupied with his future prospects in this life. He was poor, and meant to support himself by teaching, and said that without he learnt French he could not possibly obtain a situation as a tutor.

Some friends, to please his fancy, brought him French books, with a dictionary and grammar. From morning till evening the poor fellow never ceased from study, and all through the night I used to hear him muttering French words without intermission in a strange, false accent; whether he was dreaming or waking I cannot tell: he was very impatient if interrupted for a moment, and highly displeased if any one inquired how he felt—he said it was not fair to interfere with his study. I used to watch him, and his situation made me shudder, and revived serious thoughts which had been forgotten since my earlier years. I had life and health in prospect, and my hopeful aspirations after knowledge and distinction were but little damped by any anxious thoughts of the uncertainty of providing for my support; yet I was overpowered by the solemn thought that all my strivings too would end in death as certainly, if not so soon, as the poor student's, and the struggle between the claims of science and religion, which I thought had ended, recommenced.

One day the poor invalid studied more eagerly than ever he seemed to work in haste; he whispered the forms rapidly over to himself, and sought with hurried fingers and a look of eager anxiety for the words he wanted: towards evening he seemed exhausted, but still pursued his work. I could not take my eyes from watching him. Some medical students passed through the ward. I begged them to observe his state, and asked if they would send a clergyman. They approached him and inquired how he felt. "Perfectly well," he said, "only very tired by my studies; I must sleep a little and then begin again."

They whispered as they passed that the poor sufferer might live a few days longer, and to send a minister might hurry and destroy him. I only shook my head and placed myself upon the bed so that he could not see me. He seemed to slumber for a time and then to make an effort to resume his work; his hand still grasped the book, but had not power to turn the leaves: his head sank on the pillow,—I heard a slight rattle in the throat—and then his last sigh.

I left the hospital cured, but I was alone and felt forsaken; my two brothers were not in Copenhagen, I had no friend but my uncle, and he received me kindly. I had not yet openly determined on the choice of a profession, and the time was come when I must declare it. Professor Bang had taken it for I granted that I was studying for the ministry—my own determination was for science. I felt averse to the theology which was then in vogue in Denmark: it was a mixture of stiff orthodoxy and low rationalism which neutralized each other; the one was received without belief, the other without examination. I still had strong religious feelings, and preserved them as a hidden treasure; but I held them as impressions, not as subjects for investigation.

I thought myself incapable of following the subtle disputations of dogmatical learning, while my whole mind was absorbed in the love of natural philosophy. When I confessed that I meant to devote myself to science, my uncle's vexation was extreme. "You possess nothing at all," he said, "and yet you want to play the gentleman." I saw plainly that he thought it quite superfluous to take individual fitness into consideration in the choice of a profession. Nothing remained for me, therefore, but to resolve to convince him by my industry that I had chosen right.

Many men of high authority in science had entertained great hopes of my success; but before my conduct could be proved or those hopes realized, much time must elapse, and in that time I must be sup-ported and my education finished. My difficulties were immense, and I should no doubt have sunk beneath their weight like many others, had not my good uncle determined, in spite of his displeasure, that his promise to protect me which he had given to his sister in her dying hour should be redeemed.

Henceforth I became a member of my uncle's family, and he provided for all my wants. His stepsons, the Mynsters, were my friends, and I rejoiced to join a very cultivated and intellectual society of young men; at the same time I seized every opportunity to help myself. I assisted to prepare the students for examination, gave lessons on several elementary parts of science, and contributed to a journal. I was sometimes rich according to my own ideas, and all that I could spare was spent in books or specimens. My few vexations were but passing shadows, and I always think of that period of my life with satisfaction: it occupied the time from the autumn of 1792 to the spring of 1794, being from my nineteenth to my twentieth year. Most of the members of our circle were older than myself, and have lived out their day; two only of the more distinguished are still living, (at time of first publication)—Mynster, Bishop of Siaelland, Professor Bang's youngest stepson, and Horneman, the professor of botany.

I passed a good examination in all branches of natural philosophy, but I was distinguished in mineralogy. Towards the close of my attendance at the university I began to suffer both in health and spirits; a society offered me a commission to visit the western coasts of Norway for the purpose of collecting specimens and making scientific researches, and I determined to accept it. I was not without misgivings on the subject of expense, for the small sum to be paid in advance by my employers would be nearly consumed in preparations for the voyage, and my only property consisted in a tolerable library and a good collection of mineral specimens. Youth is, however, apt to overlook impending difficulties, and my longing desire to explore the treasures of the mountains, joined to the hope of regaining health and energy by the excursion, overcame every prudent fear.

We sailed with a favourable wind, but it changed, and we took refuge in a small harbour a few miles south of Stavanger, my birthplace. As we approached the coast the rocks rose, perpendicularly and rugged from the sea, and we sailed between high crags into the secluded harbour. Nothing was visible but water and bare mountains, except here and there a fisher's hut, and one small green patch among the rocks, in the midst of which stood a handsome house; it belonged to a merchant who was tempted by the herring fishery to make an abode in that dreary region; he received us with great hospitality while we remained there wind-bound.

At length we left the harbour, and on the second night found ourselves in the intricate and wonderful mazes of the rocky Archipelago of the western coast of Norway. The passage to Bergen, to which place we were bound, lies among those islands. My impatience would not let me sleep, and in the twilight of the night (for there was no longer any real darkness) I stood upon the deck and gazed upon the masses of steep rugged rock which surrounded us on every side. The day came on, thick and misty; it rained fast; the mountains were enveloped in the mist, but here and there huge dark masses rose above it, while we heard the raging sea dash against their bases: for a short time I regretted that the heavy atmosphere veiled the outline from our sight, but there was something so mysteriously grand in nature thus veiling her secrets and revealing them by degrees, that I abandoned myself wholly to the sublime impression.

The weather cleared towards noon; immense heights of sharp dark walls of rock stood sometimes suddenly uncovered close before us, or the sweeping clouds opened, and at an amazing altitude we saw the rugged summit of a mountain which rose above the lower mist, and seemed to be poised free in the midair. We felt a crushing sense of the immensity of the mountains which surrounded us, as the south-west wind drove mist and clouds together towards the sea, and the amazing scene lay in the clear sunshine open to our view.

There is nothing in Europe to compare with it; the vast ocean suddenly breaks into the very bosom of the mountains, whose shattered sides rise in many places from 4000 to 5000 feet perpendicularly from the water. The rocky islands seem torn and broken through, and stand up in sharp peaks from the sea. As we sailed among them we observed that soon after all around was bathed in sunshine, the craggy sides seemed to detain some lingering clouds which hovered for an instant on their summits, or girdled round them and then flew off to follow the great mass of vapour in the western sky.

Sometimes we threaded through a narrow pass, again we found ourselves on a wide expanse of water like a lake, encompassed by dark cliffs; then the mountains opened, and we glanced into a valley green with mossy vegetation. At one time we sailed along a wall of rock; the water there was still, and so translucent that we could see the rock beneath it for an immense depth as clearly as that above us. Before us, and at an immense height we perceived a curved line like a thread illummated by the sun; it stretched from the cliff above, and bent down towards the sea. It was a waterfall which sprang forward from the mountain; there was no apparent motion,—it was simply fixed dazzling arch; and the water was dissipated, and every trace of vapour lost in the pure atmosphere, before it reached the sea we sailed beneath it.

We were two days and as many brilliant nights making our passage through the islands. On the morning of the third we saw a row of white buildings on the brow of some lower hills, they were warehouses, indicating our approach to Bergen.

My apprehensions of being in distress for funds proved far from groundless, and my situation became daily more embarrassing. At length, in the middle of July, I received a small remittance, by means of which I hired a boat and proper apparel to fish for the *mollusca*, to collect and examine specimens which was a principal object of my mission. I passed six weeks on the wild coast, suffering many hardships and privations: yet it was a period of enjoyment.

At Sogne-Fjord I explored the deep ravines where rocks on either side stand to the height of several thousand feet. The sea rushes up those dark narrow chasms, into the depths of which the sun only reaches for an hour or two even in the height of summer. It is dangerous to venture up them in a boat, for the mountain torrents bring down huge blocks of stone which are projected from the brink of the precipice above into the gulf beneath.

I visited Leierdals-Oven, near Sogne-Fjord, and beheld all the enchantments of the south enclosed in the rude grandeur of northern mountain scenery; the bitter storms of winter never penetrate into those peaceful valleys, but expend their power on the surrounding summits. The snow melts into rain before it falls, and when the summer sun visits them it brings the genial atmosphere of southern climates, while the vegetation remains perpetually fresh from the moisture which descends from the hills above. I have described the scenery and the incidents of that deeply interesting time in my novel of *The Four Norwegians*.

I found myself once more in my poor room at Bergen, a prey to pressing anxieties, both in regard to my immediate wants and to my future course in life. I had gathered many new and valuable specimens in the course of my excursions, but I failed in the means to compare them and arrange my treasures, and I felt far from satisfied with the result of my geological examination of the country. I was in perplexity, and almost in despair; no support came to me at that time in the pious trust which had so brightened the earlier years of childhood—such consolation was forgotten or seemed extinguished.

I felt at length that I must make some strong resolve. I considered that my journey had proved all but fruitless, and that with the miserable results I dared not present myself again in Copenhagen. The idea then occurred to me of going first to Germany; that country was the scene of a vast intellectual development, and I was attracted by the new philosophy which was struggling for existence. Kant was already known to me, and I longed to participate in the dawning light. I thought that if I were to win distinction in Germany, I could afterwards return to Denmark; the result of my researches in Norway could in the meantime be more effectually arranged in Hamburg, and my friends should receive their first communication from that place.

I forgot or undervalued the difficulty I must contend again in my imperfect knowledge of the German language; I knew that I must suffer much, that want and fatigue might lay me on a bed of sickness—but I was resolved. I must not omit to confess an act partaking strangely of mixed power and weakness, with which I sealed my final determination. In order to prove my strength to meet the hour of trial I held my finger in the flame of the light which stood by me, and kept it firmly there until the wound was deep, I was strengthened by the ordeal, though the after-suffering cost me many sleepless nights.

Among those who had attached themselves to me in my forlorn state in Bergen was a prosperous young merchant; he had learnt my wish to go to Hamburg, knew my circumstances an proposed to me to undertake the charge of a cargo which he was going to send, saying that my percentage would produce a considerable sum. Knowing my natural unfitness for any kind of business I felt compelled to decline the offer, grateful as I was for I could not but perceive that it had been made only with a view to aid me.

He pressed his kindness on me, and it was after a sleepless night that I finally resisted the temptation. I accepted a sum of money which he generously offered and which would pay my travelling and immediate expenses. I had sanguine hopes that the knowledge I had acquired would serve me well in Germany, and I wrote to my friends in Copenhagen to my books and specimens, which I fancied, even parted with below their value, would relieve me from all my liabilities and leave me a considerable sum.

CHAPTER 3

Voyage to Hamburg

We sailed from Bergen in a brig on the 15th of October; we were detained by contrary winds, and it was not till the end of November that we actually commenced our voyage to cross the North Sea in that stormy season. Our captain was ignorant and uncivil, and after being driven towards the coast of Scotland and encountering many storms we found ourselves at last at the mouth of the Elbe. It was very heavy weather, and the gale drove us into the river. Towards evening we tried to anchor, but without success; the brig drove, she struck, the masts were carried away, and she remained a perfect wreck.

I left the sinking ship in the last boat with fifteen men, and in the night we were carried by the current four or five miles out into the open sea. I was so exhausted that I felt scarcely sensible of our danger, for I had helped during many days to work the ship, and had just fallen asleep in the cabin when she struck, and I lay all night, half-unconscious in the bottom of the boat while the waves dashed over us. In the morning a frigate picked us up.

I had a large Newfoundland dog on board with me; it was faithful creature, ever ready to protect me in case of danger: it was left in the ship, and I was grieved to think that I had lost him. When, however, we had been some little time on board the frigate, I heard a splashing at the side—it was my dog. Could he have followed us on the open sea that stormy night, and had he seen the frigate in the morning and made towards it? I could not tell, but it pleased me to believe that he had been guided by his love for me, and I felt bound to return his attachment, though I knew not how I should support him; I had in fact lost everything. The small sum I had brought with me in cash had been nearly consumed by paying my passage and expenses on the voyage; my draft upon the merchant in Hamburg was lost with all my other property, and even my good watch was left in the cabin when I sprang up hastily on the striking of the ship.

I left the hotel in Hamburg, in which we had taken refuge upon landing, found my way into the town, and crept into a small garret. It was a brilliant time for the city. Pichegru had won a series of successes in Belgium; Holland was open to him, and a number of Dutch refugees of the first families had crowded into Hamburg. A vast influx of trade and riches was the consequence of the shutting up of other ports. I sought out the merchant L———, on whom the bill which I had lost was drawn. I told my history and named the sum, and to my surprise and great relief he paid me instantly. He had already received letters from his friend at Bergen preparing him to see me and he knew also of the shipwreck. He was not among the higher class of merchants, nor was he a man of cultivation but he received me most kindly, asked me to his plain but hospitable table and was dissatisfied when I stayed away.

Under my circumstances there was little chance of study; the unfulfilled task of communicating with the society which had sent me to Norway was a heavy burden on my mind. I had lost all my collection and my books, and instead of a scientific report, I had the bare story of my shipwreck to detail. I feared my excuse would seem like a fiction. True, I had witnesses in Bergen of the diligence with which I had worked. I wrote to beg their testimony; but still the daring, thoughtless step which I had taken in thus throwing myself helpless into a foreign land seemed, even to myself, so like a foolish dream, that I could hardly hope my friends would understand the motives which had governed me. I wrote and entreated them to sell my books and property in Copenhagen; their answers happily contained no doubts of my integrity, but they stated the great difficulty disposing of my property, and the fear that, by a forced sale, they would produce so small a sum that it would aid me little.

In the meantime my resources dwindled fearfully—I could not work, I only tried to forget my cares in the ever-varying scenes of the great city.

It was a fine winter—the snow covered the ground; my small garret was hired only by the week, my poor wardrobe was easily made into a small package, and so taking all my possessions with me I went forth on a wandering excursion. I expected to supply my moderate wants more cheaply in the country than I could in Hamburg, and my faithful dog followed me as friend and protector. It was partly on his account that I had determined to quit the city, for, obliged as I was to restrict my outlay to the uttermost, I found his daily food a severe expense. I wandered among towns and villages, avoiding only the direction of Rendsburg, where my father lived, and so came at length to the fortress of Glückstadt. I lingered there, tempted by the kindness of the host of the small inn at which I stopped; they were poor people, and had lost their property by a bankruptcy, and their only child had perished in Greenland. It seemed a comfort to them to condole with me when I related my shipwreck and misfortunes, and to receive my sympathy on their still heavier sorrows.

The wall of the castle and a large moat were near the inn. Dogs were forbidden to be upon the works, and I had many fears about my faithful Newfoundlander. One day I wandered out, thinking over my trials and those of my poor host, when I heard a shot. I hardly know why I was seized with such alarm. My dog had followed me. I did not see him: I called, but he did not come, and I perceived the mark of his feet where he had clambered up the wall. I had already engaged the sentinel, by small present, to be careful of my dog; he now approached me sorrowfully; he had seen only just a portion of the poor dog's back as he leaped among the snow; he had not recognized him, and he had fired. I found the poor animal— he licked my hand, and died.

All my circumstances must be remembered to understand how terribly I felt the loss; my kind host sympathized with me, but could stay no longer there. I paid him, and the reckoning was so trifling that I could not but perceive that the good people merely made a charge to save my feelings.

I went forth again without my friend and returned to Hamburg. I felt indescribably forsaken. The little daily self-denials which I had been obliged to make for my poor dog's sake had been an interest to me, and it seemed as if fate closed on me when I lost the last living thing which was attached to me. I had passed two wasted months— my very intellects seemed failing under my despair.

I returned to Hamburg. My friend L——— welcomed me; with joy, and his wife and sister overwhelmed me with questions! and reproaches that I had quitted them so suddenly; they had looked for me in vain, and suffered many fears on my account. I told them all, and then the merchant asked to speak to me, alone. How great was my amazement when he proposed to me to learn his business! "I have not been blind," he said, "to your regard for my sister." His plan was all arranged: I was to marry the sister, and in due time become his partner.

I was shocked at the mistake, and terrified with the fear of wounding the feelings of those who had been so good to me The sister was much older than I; she was far from being attractive, and her defective education had allowed us little opportunity of conversation. No sentiment deeper than a thankful return for kindness had ever crossed my mind, nor do I think that she had any warmer preference for myself.

In such perplexing moments a sort of instinct frequently avails more than hours of reflection. I saw instantly that the two parts of the proposal were conditionally annexed to each other. I represented, therefore, the impossibility of accepting the first I urged my belief that the assistance of my friends would relieve me from the existing distress, which I regarded merely as temporary, and I dwelt on my utter incapacity for business, and my still absorbing love of science, and I so brought the first condition under prominent consideration, that the second was but distantly and delicately alluded to. I succeeded so well that retreated from my dilemma without in the least falling in my kind friend's estimation.

L——'s father-in-law proposed to me to leave the hotel where I had passed the first evening after my return, and hire a smart room in a house belonging to him, at a very trifling rent—it was again a garret. I passed three or four weeks there, my circumstances darkening daily, and my letters from Copenhagen bringing no prospect of relief. As my want increased I abstained from visiting either the L—— family or a Danish friend from whom I had also received kindness. I lived for eight days on fruit and bread; at length I had no money left, and I was very ill. The house in which I lived was a public-house, frequented by sailors and persons of indifferent character.

I returned one evening to my room, feeling extremely ill, when, as I passed by the open door of a room, I saw that it was lighted up and that dancing was going on. I retreated to my bed and fell into a dreamy, feverish sort of sleep; I was still aware of the music and the noisy mirth, and they drove me almost to distraction; about midnight I heard no more music, but the uproar had increased, and as I waked I heard footsteps on the stairs, and a crowd of drunken persons broke into my room and fought furiously by my bed; the people of the house came and restored order, but I believe I should have perished in that last extremity had not my kind friends sought me out that same day and succoured me with every aid which benevolence and medical skill could give me.

My proud spirit was at length subdued. I saw that I could not stay in Hamburg; my father was living not far off at Rendsburg, and I resolved to write and tell him all. I had been previously advised by my friends in Copenhagen to go to Kiel, and there, by teaching or by giving public lectures, to try to gain a living; why I did not adopt that course whilst some little money still remained at my command I cannot tell, but now that I had expended all I wrote to entreat my father to receive me until I might be supplied from Copenhagen with means to enable me to go to Kiel. I knew my father: reproaches such as I felt I well deserved, formed no part of his reply. He wrote—

My last bread will I share with thee—hasten hither, for I long for thee.

I was soon at Rendsburg with my poor father; his own circumstances were sadly reduced, and it was a bitter punishment to me to feel that I was obliged to increase his burdens. Yet he tried to make me forget my own misfortunes and to believe that my presence was a comfort to him; he still clung to the hopes which he had once built upon my opening powers, and held firm to the belief that success was yet before me, and while I waited in continual disappointment for the expected remittance from Copenhagen, he comforted and encouraged me; my brothers also treated me most kindly, especially the younger, who was quartered in the garrison as a subaltern; we spent our time together in mutual improvement, and I felt once more happy in returning energy for study and renewed confidence in my own powers.

We lived in great retirement, but very happily, and I felt quite equal to endure the only small misfortune which was reserved to complete the wreck of my former fortunes. News arrived from Copenhagen that my last remaining property had perished; my friends had been actually negotiating a sale of my books and cabinets of natural history to the Crown Prince, the present king of Denmark, then ten years old, but before it was completed a fire broke out in the building where they had been deposited and they were all consumed. On the other hand a pleasant though trifling incident occurred to cheer my hopes and justify my father's partial faith in my future career: a number of the *Literary Gazette* appeared, in which some work of mine was highly praised, and it was a great joy to me to see my father's satisfaction.

A whole year passed while I was recovering my usual vigour both of mind and body, and it was then determined that I should try whether my talents would avail me in the University of Kiel, and I was furnished with an introduction from Professor Bahl in Copenhagen to Professor Fabricius at Kiel. I possessed five dollars when I left Rendsburg to begin my new career.

I arrived in Kiel in February, 1796; two years had passed since I had quitted Copenhagen, and I felt that I was beginning a new epoch of my life. I was not without fear of my success but my resolutions were strong to turn every hour to the best account. Fabricius was already known to me as the first entomologist of his day; I waited on him and was prepossessed by his appearance: he was a little, benevolent-looking man, and received me joyfully, as if he had expected me: "Your engagements in the university," he said, "can begin only with the next term; in the meantime you must live; there are here many families who wish their children to be instructed in natural history; the receipts will be but moderate, but they will assist you till we can appoint you to some more important office."

This was happiness indeed! I entered upon my new duties with gratitude and hope, and soon found that four or five hours daily, employed in teaching, furnished me with sufficient for my wants. I had access to the library of the university and pursued my studies with avidity, rejoicing in the consciousness of, strengthening and expanding intellect.

I enjoyed the society of many men of science, who received me with the utmost kindness. I must relate the circumstances of my first introduction to the learned Professor Cramer, since they were truly original. He had a country-house in the suburbs, and when I called to pay my respects I was told I should find him in his garden. I heard the sound of laughter and merry voices as I approached, and saw an elderly gentleman bent forwards in the middle of a walk, while several boys were playing leap-frog over him; a lady who stood by him said, as soon as she perceived me, "Cramer, Steffens is there."

"Well," he said, without moving, "leap then." I was delighted with the new mode of introduction to a man of science, took my leap clean over him, and then turned round to make my bow and compliments. He was delighted, and as my good leap also won the hearts of the young people, I was at once admitted as an acquaintance in the happy circle. Notwithstanding this quaint reception, Cramer was a man of deep reflection with all the quiet manner of a true philosopher.

My lectures began under flattering circumstances: the number of students at the university did not exceed three hundred, and above seventy put down their names to attend my class. I had claimed no entrance fees, being at first timid about expressing my subject well in a language with which I was not perfectly familiar; I had not, however, lectured many weeks, before a very considerable sum was forwarded to me by the class collectively as a testimony of their value of my teaching. I hesitated for a moment whether I should accept it, but I reflected that it would be unwise to let false pride induce me to reject such well-meant kindness: the sum was very welcome, and my acceptance cemented my connection with the givers, for it is a part of human nature to value all things according to the degree of sacrifice which has been made to obtain them. I have observed that unpaid lecturers are rarely carefully attended.

In April, 1797, I took my degree. The dean of the faculty of Philosophy did me the honour to celebrate the occasion, and nearly all the professors were present; and having at length established some reputation as an author and university lecturer, in a language new to me, I felt that I might once more present myself without disgrace before my Copenhagen friends. The conditions which I laid upon myself in Bergen, to win some degree of reputation before I would again appear amongst them, seemed fulfilled; for my German work on the study of mineralogy, fully sensible as I was of its deficiencies, encouraged me to believe that I should eventually take the place I so much coveted amongst the authors of Germany.

They were brilliant, happy days which I then passed in Copenhagen, retracing scenes of past enjoyment, and reviving early friendships. My kind Uncle Bang still maintained his former confidence in my powers and my ultimate success in life, and even the Society in whose service I had gone to Norway assumed the blame of my misfortunes for having supplied my wants so scantily. After a few weeks I returned to my small study and my course of duties in the university of Kiel.

I was tempted by the lovely scenery of Holstein, and by the shady woods which surrounded Kiel, to make many rambles. One beech wood was my favourite haunt. It was bathed on one side by the sea, and on the other bounded by the hills; the foliage was so rich, the green so tender, the shades so peacefully retired, that Siaelland and all its magic loveliness seemed to rise again before me. When I wandered in the plains there was but one defect to spoil the pleasure of an excursion.

The high hedges or fences, called in Holstein "redder," hide the view and shade the roads, so that even in the finest summer weather they are seldom dry; it is only where the ground ascends that the rich landscape is perceived, and the luxuriant fields, each bounded by its living fence, look like so many highly cultivated gardens. I was pleased with the rough and simple-mannered peasantry, and with their cheerful cottages, strangely neat and scrupulously clean, though the cows and oxen live under the same roof with the family. When the large doors are opened, and through the rows of cows and horses standing in the dark on each side, the kitchen hearth is seen beyond, the smoke curling up into the roof, which is the only chimney, and all the brightly polished brass and copper kitchen utensils, of which there is always a superabundance, shining in the distance, the effect is very singular and pleasing.

In the western part of Holstein the peasantry were small, independent proprietors of the land. A little incident struck me as being very characteristic of their manners. I was in the marshes near Wilster, the place whence my family originally came, and a young lawyer of my acquaintance proposed to introduce me to one of those independent countrymen who possessed a large property. I entered the room, where a fat peasant was sitting, his head covered by a three-cornered hat. I was named to him; he just raised his hat, and put it on again, nodded familiarly to me, and offered me a glass of wine. After some hesitation I received the glass, when he looked at me with a good-natured, pitying sort of smile, and said in the *platt* Deutsch, "It is a good while, I fancy, since you have been so lucky as to taste wine." The Holstein peasant, in his proud, self-satisfied reserve, is a contrast to the frank, generous, and cheerful Norwegian, who is, however, fully conscious of his independence.

The opposition between the aristocracy and the liberally disposed middle classes was strong in Holstein at that time. The progress of education it is true occasioned a degree of communication between the nobles and the *burgher* class, but there was no cordiality on either side. Holstein was then the centre of a literature which was influential throughout Germany. Lessing, during his residence in Hamburg, had enlightened Holstein by his powerful mind; the original thinker Claudius lived in Wandsbeck; Boye in Muldorf, as well as the celebrated aged Niebuhr; the severe Rector Boss ruled not only in the schools at Euten, but through all the province; and Klopstock and Goethe were at that time honoured there, as they were later throughout Germany.

I made a new acquaintance—one who had the most important influence on me, and brought me at once into the midst of the intellectual flood which was pouring on in Germany—it was with Rist. He came from Jena, where he had heard *Fichte*. Henceforward, though I held independent views, I belonged to a circle of young men who were in some sense the followers of Fichte.

I was summoned to Rendsburg in consequence of the dangerous illness of my father. My improved position was the last comfort which cheered his life of trial. He had shared in my anxieties at Rendsburg, and felt for my humiliation without uttering a reproach, and he seemed afterwards to have outlived the sense of his own misfortunes in the triumph of my success at Kiel; it is impossible to sum up all that I owe to his having so spared me in his tenderness. I found him in the last extremity, and a few hours later I received his last breath and closed his eyes.

Travelling was always the great object of my wishes, and there was no country in Europe where so much assistance was granted to young men of promise, whether in art or scientific pursuits, to improve themselves by travel, as in Denmark. Many of my former friends, aided by such funds, had passed through Kiel, and they had excited my own hopes of being similarly fortunate. By Hensler's kind assistance my desire was made known to Count Schimmelmann, and I was shortly afterwards desired to wait upon him in Copenhagen. I there found that my friend Rist, who was living in Count Schimmelmann's house, had, as I suspected, been the kind promoter of my wishes; he also obtained for me a reception there, and for the first time in my life I was received into the private circle of one of the highest personages in the land.

Count Schimmelmann, then minister of finance, was remarkable both for his political career and his great literary genius and attainments. He was born a poet, and had a mind open to the allurements of speculative philosophy. The day which I passed in his charming villa, Söelyst, where he encouraged me to lay before him even my yet unripened thoughts or the great views which were then dawning on the world of science and metaphysics, were among the brightest of my life. They lasted three weeks, and ended by the fulfilment of my most ardent wish. Sufficient funds were granted me, together with the permission to travel in Germany in company with the celebrated botanist Horneman.

CHAPTER 4

Departure for Denmark

Mineralogy being the subject on which I had earned my chief reputation in Copenhagen, I knew that I should be expected to proceed at once to Freiburg, which was then the great school of Europe for that science; but I felt it impossible to pass. by unvisited those scenes where the great intellectual strength of Germany was in progress of development. I lingered a short time both at Jena and at Weimar on my way to the Thuringian mining district; but it was not till after my return that the bright hopes of many years were realized in my intercourse with the great spirits of the age.

On my second visit to Jena, Schelling had just returned from Leipzig, and was beginning a course of lectures. I found students and professors all crowded together to listen to him. Schelling had a most youthful look—he was in fact two years younger than myself; and yet of all the men whose fame attracted me, it was he whom I most longed to know. His manner was decided, with almost an air of defiance; he had large cheek-bones, a high forehead, and wide temples; his countenance was full of energetic self-possession as he stood with his head thrown slightly back and his full clear eye beaming with power. He spoke of the necessity of understanding Nature in her simple oneness (*Einheit*)—of the light which would make all things clear were they viewed from the point of sight of unity and reason (*Vernunft*).

He carried my feelings on with him, and I went the same day to visit him; he received me not only kindly, but with joy. I was the first who, being devoted to a particular department of natural history, was willing to seize and carry out his view. My coincidence of thought with Schelling filled me with a confidence which almost bounded on presumption

I went from Schelling to Fichte. He was short and robust in figure, but had a searching, commanding look; he made use of most keenly sharp expressions, while he tried by every imaginable means to make his meaning understood, being fully aware of the slender powers of too many of his hearers. He seemed to claim imperiously a strict obedience of thought, forbidding the suspicion of a doubt. "Gentlemen," he began "compose yourselves; turn your thoughts inwards; we have nothing to do now with anything external, but simply with ourselves."

The audience so commanded, seemed each to do his best to retreat within himself: some changed their position and sat bolt upright, some curled themselves up and shut their eyes, all waited breathlessly for the next word. "Gentlemen, let your thought be—the Wall." I perceived that the listeners did all they could to possess their minds fully with the wall, and they seemed to succeed. "Now have you thought—the wall. Now, gentlemen, let your thought be,—that which thought the wall." It was curious to watch the evident perplexity and distress.

Many seemed to search about in vain without the power of forming any idea of "what had thought the wall," and I quite understood how many young minds which could so stumble on the threshold of speculative philosophy might be in danger of falling into a most unhealthy state by striving further. Fichte's lecture, however, was most admirable, distinct, and lucid, and I never heard any exposition at all to be compared with it. Fichte made few philosophers, but many powerful reasoners...

My thorough acquaintance with Goethe delighted A. W. Schlegel and his gifted wife, in whose society I spent much time. They asked me once to read part of the *Faust*, being curious to hear how Goethe's verse would sound in my rough northern accent. The book was not at hand, and I went on from memory, reciting passage after passage as they referred to them. Their pleasure was so great that it was determined that I should forthwith be introduced to the great poet. Another friend, however, anticipated this intention, and I felt as if a momentous event were taking place when I first stood forward in Goethe's presence.

I was obliged instantly to turn away, for tears gushed involuntarily into my eyes. A cruel mortification, however, followed: it was natural perhaps for me to fancy that he must know the feelings which I cherished towards him; he however turned with indifference to another stranger who was introduced at the same time, and I did not receive the slightest notice. He was yet in the prime of life; the well-bred calmness of his manner began to be tiresome, even vexatious to me; I recalled the many histories which were current of his pride and cold condescension, and went home in a most unamiable state of feeling. I hastened the next day to Schlegel; his wife seemed terrified when she heard the bitterness with which I spoke of Goethe, but my northern pride and obstinacy were aroused: the more I had honoured, almost worshipped him, the more I felt determined that I never would be twice presented to him.

Many weeks passed over; I tried to lose myself in study, but though my mind was active, a sense as of some great misfortune oppressed me still. At length the celebrated anatomist Loder proposed to give a party on his birthday. A play was to be acted: *The Actor against his Will* was chosen, and I was asked to fill the principal part. The part contains many declamatory passages from various authors, chosen from old plays of no great merit, and to increase the interest I introduced instead several from the plays of Iffland and Schiller.

When we were assembled for the last rehearsal Goethe appeared amongst us, much to my surprise, for his intention of being present had been concealed from me. When he had spoken to the ladies, he came up to me with all the kind manner of an old acquaintance. "I have hoped long," he said, "to see you at my house in Weimar; I have much to talk with you about, much to tell you. After a few days will you return with me?"

What happiness! At length I felt that I was at home in Jena; my joy was reflected in the spirit which I threw into my performance. Goethe gave much good advice, and I thought the dramatic scene in 'Wilhelm Meister' was acted in reality. When I came to the part where I was to declaim a passage from Schiller, he came up kindly and said, "Choose from another author—we had rather that our good friend Schiller were let alone."

I substituted a speech from Kotzebue . . . .

I was in Jena when Fichte was denounced through Reinhart by order of the Saxon Court, under the charge of atheism. I was greatly excited against what appeared to me an invasion of the right of free inquiry. I took an active part in getting up a petition from the students against the banishment of Fichte from the university. In subsequent more dispassionate seasons of reflection I have inquired doubtingly whether the charge was wholly groundless. I went to Halle and was there introduced to Reichardt by Schlegel and by Goethe, both of whom had recently been reconciled to him, and I entered for the first time the hospitable family, every member of which at once excited a powerful interest.

The daughter, who was afterwards to be my wife, was not at that time at home. Reichardt met me with the open frankness which was peculiar to him, but my feeling was not then in his favour. The part he had taken in the French revolution, his intimacy with the leader, and his democratic opinions, had excited the displeasure of the Court of Berlin, and Goethe had been so incensed as to refuse to listen to Reichardt's musical composition to his own words. Schlegel shared in the same displeasure, and they had only both been lately reconciled, my prepossessions therefore were against him when I first entered his charming dwelling, and was led by him into his little park, which I thought the most perfect of his compositions.

I travelled alone from Frankfort to Bamberg. I had introductions to Röschlaub, Marcus, and Professor Paulus, who expected me. I took the whim to enter the place unattended carrying my own portman-teau, and when I arrived at the hotel there was much bustle, it being the annual fair. The host and all the waiters were busy, and in answer to my application for a room I obtained only a hasty reply that there was none for me. On repeating my demand a miserable garret was offered to me. I made a display of my purse and was insisting on a better lodg-ing, when a servant entered and inquired if Dr. Steffens arrived.

The waiter answered with a regretful "No;" I declared my identity, and great was my amazement at the sudden change which instantly took place. I found that I was expected at the hotel, and I was over-whelmed with excuses and civilities. When I shortly afterwards paid a visit to Professor Paulus, I learnt that my name might well be held in high respect by the waiter, for the great room had been engaged for the following day to celebrate my arrival by a dinner, at which all the professors, principal inhabitants, and students were to be present.

It was the first time in my life that such public testimony of respect had ever been accorded me; I was a proud and happy man that day, when I took my place between the wife of Paulus and the niece of Marcus, and when two of the most celebrated physicians in all Ger-many spoke of their respect for me in terms which made me feel both honoured and ashamed. Yet when I retired alone into my chamber I felt that the whole scene was overwrought, and not justified by any reputation which I had yet earned. I was unable to feel perfect satisfac-tion, but a thought passed over me how, all unfit as I esteemed myself, it might have proved a subject of unmixed rejoicing.

I thought of my father's prophetic trust in my future, and of all his partial hopes; I thought how he had upheld and comforted me in misery; I fancied myself once more in our small room in Rendsburg, living in poverty and seclusion, but supported by his indulgence and encouragement; and I thought how should I have rejoiced indeed in honour if I could have imparted it to him. Thus did my day of triumph end in an agony of tears.

I saw the last century expire in Jena, and I passed the first evening of the new one in Weimar, at a masquerade given by the Court. A representation composed by Goethe commenced the evening, and towards midnight I joined Goethe, Schiller, and Schelling in a retired *boudoir*, where we passed some brilliant hours. The year begun thus cheerfully was closed in solitude, amongst the grand and lonely wilds of Tharand, exploring the treasures of the mines. I had passed the summer alternately in Dresden and in Tharand; and when I recall the scenes of that year I must regard it as the richest of my life; it was so both in enjoyment and in promise, for I had met with Reichardt's youngest daughter, who was to be afterwards my wife; she had come with her grandmother to visit Tieck's wife, her aunt, at Dresden; the grandmother was the daughter of Alberti, so well known in Hamburg for his literary productions as well as for his preaching.

The reputation I had earned in Germany obtained for me the honour of an invitation to take part in a new college, which was intended to be established in Ireland, the chief object of which was to be the study of geognosy, for the benefit of the mining, interests. Disciples of the Wernerian school were sought for, and Mohs, Herder and I were offered appointments. I was especially desired to undertake the literary department.

The prospect of a sufficient income and active employment, though in a country so remote from all my former ties, had many powerful inducements for me, and even the dim uncertainty of the whole future mode of life added an attractive charm: after many inward struggles, however, I felt unable to expatriate myself so utterly; my hopes still turned towards my Fatherland, my most eager desire was to impart the treasures in philosophy and science which I had so lately gathered to my own countrymen, and I still trusted that Count Schimmelmann's partiality would procure me leave to lecture in Copenhagen and some honourable and useful means of support.

I left Tharand with regret, and took leave with still deeper sorrow of Dresden, where amongst many friends, I had become especially attached to Tieck and his kind family. I passed hastily through Leipzig, for it was at Giedichtenstein that my fate was to be decided. Reichardt was absent; and though I was full of confidence that my suit would prosper, I had yet some anxious days to wait in Halle. He at length returned from Weimar, where he had been with Goethe. I had been talked of by them, and Goethe had thought highly of the Treatise which I had lately dedicated to him; Reichardt was therefore prepared to receive me favourably, I was invited to Giedichtenstein, I was betrothed to my young bride, and I was to be allowed to return at the expiration of a year and take her as my wife to Copenhagen.

I returned in 1802 to Copenhagen, being then in my thirtieth year: no one had enjoyed a happier youth than I, except during those two sad years of trial; and even then the firm belief that I should rise and prosper never left me. I was full of hopes when I again entered Denmark, but it was fitting that I should share the common lot of mortal disappointment. The discouragements which afterwards determined me to quit my native land met me in threatening aspect on my first return. Count Schimmelmann received me with his former kindness; he was eager to be informed of all that I had learned in Germany, and listened with deep interest whilst I laid before him the new views which had enlightened both the poetic and scientific world.

I found him scarcely prepared to enter fully into speculative philosophy; but he listened, and I won him to the cause of truth and free inquiry. I had already forwarded to him the proposal which I had received from Ireland, and he regarded it as a sufficient reason for bestowing a small but highly acceptable salary, leaving to me the arrangement of my plan of occupation. I drew up accordingly a scheme for establishing public lectures on philosophy and geognosy for the especial benefit of young men who, as clergymen or in other official situations, were intended for a secluded life among the mountain districts of Norway.

I also proposed to make an annual excursion to those districts, to visit the students as they became established, and regulate their system of research and study. The Count approved; and had I depended upon him alone for the means of carrying out my scheme, I might have attained an enviable position.

The chief mover at that time in all subjects pertaining to national education was the Duke von Augustenburg, brother-in-law to the King. He partook very violently of the dislike which prevailed against German opinions, with the meaning of which he, like the public in general, was wholly unacquainted. I have to regret some injudicious expressions with which I met his prejudices when I was admitted to an audience; the interview convinced me that even if he did not oppose my lecturing, he would afford no assistance to my further plans.

My views were also discouraged by one of the ministers. Count Reventlaw, to whose practical wisdom Denmark owes much of , her prosperity, but who was the declared enemy of all philosophic speculations. He held that men of science were unfit for any useful work; it was the people's happiness alone that should be cared for; religion had its uses, but should be left entirely to the clergy, and the simpler it was taught the better. When I applied I to him to appoint the time and means for my tour in Norway, he answered that he knew no use a philosopher could be of there, and took the opportunity of regretting the sinister influence which my teaching might have on the minds of the rising generation.

The difficulties which encompassed me took sometimes a ludicrous turn, and a little piece which I assisted some friends to get up at a private theatre bore no unapt allusion to my position. It was called *Erasmus Montanus*, and the plot was as follows. A student, the son of a countryman, lately returned from the university, had thrown the whole village into consternation by his logic, and pedantic assertion of truths as yet unheard-of by the poor people; the hero's bride was in despair, the parents angry, all despised him as a madman, when a recruiting office appeared, who undertook to cure him. Erasmus had just proved by a syllogism that the sexton was a hen, and his father and mother some other sort of animals, when the officer offered to argue with him for a wager. Erasmus won, and received the shilling when lo! it was listing-money. He was cured, but—he was a soldier; they had argued whether or not the world was round—what was to be done? leave father, mother, bride, everything? impossible! So he declared that the world was as flat as any pancake; peace and happiness were restored, and they all went off delighted to the wedding.

My kind and enlightened patron succeeded, notwithstanding, in obtaining me a most desirable occupation for the summer. I was commissioned to inspect the salt-mines of Oldesloe, as well as the selenite hills of Segeberg, and to report on the capability of working them to advantage. I visited my earlier friend Uncle Bang's stepson, since Bishop Münster, who was then living in his retired parsonage in Sweden, and enjoyed some days with him in recollections of former happiness; but that which I valued most in the excursion was the opportunity afforded me of making a detour to Halle, thence to fetch away my bride.

I returned through Holstein to Hamburg, and, accompanied by my wife's grandmother, proceeded to Giedichtenstein; it was in September, 1803, a few weeks after Hanover had been laid, open to the French by Count Walmoden's capitulation on the Elbe, and the country occupied by the enemy was only separate from Hamburg by that river. Notwithstanding numerous reports of danger from the soldiery, we met with no obstruction on the road. I remained a few days at Lüneburg, with a sister of my mother-in-law; the town was strongly garrisoned, and several French officers were quartered in the house where I was staying; their polished, smooth, artful manners displeased me much, and I then first felt the meaning of the misfortune which was to overshadow so many years of my life. Immediately after my marriage I returned with my young wife to Copenhagen.

I began my lectures in Copenhagen in October, 1803; my audience was large, and my success was great; not only students, but professors and men of learning and of rank and station, crowded to obtain a seat. My courage and my enthusiasm for my subject rose with my increasing popularity; but with that popularity rose also the opposition which ignorance, supported by high authority, was able to excite against me.

In the spring of 1804 I received an invitation to join the University of Halle, as professor of natural philosophy. Notwithstanding the success my lectures had obtained in Copenhagen., it was clear that they were not approved of by the government, and I felt convinced that sooner or later they would be suppressed. My desire to obtain a freer field for usefulness, joined to that of securing a sufficient and more certain means of support for my family, inclined me to accept the offered appointment. Many were the remonstrances which I was compelled to bear from friends in whose sight my departure to use my talents in a foreign land seemed a sort of treason to my own; I was urged to wait and see if brighter prospects might not tempt me to remain, but I resisted.

"If," I said, "my work should prosper, the fruit will remain in my own expanded powers, and they shall be at the service of my country should happier auspices ever encourage my return."

Chapter 5

Arrival at Halle

1804—1806

I felt the pain of departing from my country and separating from friends and kindred most severely: it was long before I could withdraw my thoughts from broken ties of earlier years, so as to permit the light of my hopeful future in a foreign land to shine on me and cheer me. I thought with sorrow that I should) hear the sweet tones of my native tongue no more, and as the fair green fields of Zealand faded from our sight, I felt as if I had abandoned myself a prey to a stranger spirit and a threatening destiny. The future, however, gradually rose again more hopefully; the German language sounded like a second mother tongue; a kind welcome awaited me from friends and relatives, and the sight of my wife's happiness aided me to master my depression.

In Lüneburg we found the hated French; the Hanoverians seemed to have submitted to the evil of their presence with a composure which incensed me to a degree that I can hardly call reasonable. We visited a French encampment near the town, and noticed the national disposition to make everything around them gay: the tents which they had seized from the Hanoverians were clean, and ornamented with flowers and wreaths, and the arms, piled up, glittered in the sunshine, while they enjoyed themselves in groups, whistling and singing. The brilliant scene filled me with a feeling of despair. An angel with a flaming sword seemed, in my imagination, to stand prepared to drive me from the paradise which I had as yet scarcely entered, and I felt the more exasperated by observing the incomprehensible indifference of the people of the land.

At Berlin all was quiet, no thought of danger was apparent, and surrounded by kind friends and relatives, we forgot our dark forebodings, and indulged in happy anticipations. I was introduced to Herr von Beyme, who was then high in favour with the King: he invited me to Potsdam, and spoke with great interest of the University of Halle, declaring his determination to do all in his power to revive and strengthen it; he hoped to see it rise to be the first seat of learning in Germany. All this from a man so high in power was most encouraging.

In September I had the happiness of seeing my wife once more restored to the society of her delighted parents, whose distress had been severe when I removed her to a distant country. Household arrangements and visits to the members of the university fully occupied my time at first, and while the requisite expenditure for beginning my establishment caused no little difficulty, I was perplexed to supply my immediate wants, and fearful that to do so I must impoverish my future means. My father-in-law had hired far too large and costly a house for me. I required a library, and though I was appointed professor of mineralogy I had no collection of specimens.

These deficiencies were, after some unpleasant contention, supplied by the university, but very inadequately, and I had to meet a great annoyance in the failure of my means in regard to salary. I had been given to expect a larger income than I had received at Copenhagen, but I had unwisely followed the opinion sent to me by Beyme through my friend Reil. They had advised me to abstain from stipulating for a fixed amount as a condition of accepting the appointment; the increase, as well as means to defray my incidental expenses, were refused me, and my financial prospects were but comfortless.

My position in regard to the university and my new colleagues as not more encouraging: one of the public prints announced that I and my wife were Catholics; another, at the same time that we were atheists; one hinted at licentious habits, another boldly affirmed that I was an opium-eater; and when I began my lectures a young professor expressed his deep commiseration for my wife, because a rapid decay of mind and early death must be the inevitable consequence of my continual excesses. In fact among the professors a general discontent at my appointment was apparent. My difficulties as lecturer on philosophy threatened to be still more serious; there were already five lecturers on the subject in the university, all of whom had obtained some degree of celebrity in authorship, and they were all united to oppose me.

By time and patience, however, more propitious signs became discernible; I found the students more prepared to receive me than the professors. Philosophy had gained much ground during the two years of my residence in Denmark, and my prospects in the reviving university were also much improved by my connection with distinguished men in each of the learned faculties Wolf, the philologist, was in his prime: his influence, derived from his profound learning, critical acumen, and keen wit, was great; and as young minds when powerfully excited on one topic become expanded to take interest in all, so Wolf's best pupils were also my most diligent attendants.

Reil was not less eminent in the faculty of medicine; his attainments in general literature were very great; he was the first medical authority of Halle and the neighbourhood, and had the largest practice as physician, in spite of an ungentle manner, which was trying to the more timid patients; I owed my appointment to his influence and he continued my firm friend to the end of his life.

I also met for the first time a man with whose friendship a new era of my life began. Schleiermacher was made a supernumerary professor about the same time that I arrived in Halle, we were soon united in most intimate confidence, and I never so, fully understood, as in my intercourse with him, that in friendships the most unlimited deference to superior judgement rather assists than destroys independent feeling. In the same way as Goethe, Schelling, and Tieck had influenced me formerly, so now did Schleiermacher; we shared our views, our thoughts, and even our likings; he was in my father-in-law Reichardt's circle as often as myself; we were companions in our walks and excursions, and the best students attended us equally, for his ethical and my philosophical teaching seemed closely connected. He was chaplain to the University.

Nearly two years passed in academic duties, and I was at length fully contented; the fairest prospects dawned upon me, and I was roused to energy by my widening field for useful endeavour. I was happy in my family, my friends, and my classes, and for the first time I was able to calculate on a sufficient provision for coming emergencies; but the ground out of which so many blessings sprang was hollow, though I knew it not.

In 1806 my daughter Clara was born, the only child whom God has preserved to me. In the spring of the same year I went to Berlin with Schleiermacher and his sister, who subsequently married Moritz Arndt. We found the city in a state of great excitement, political events had become more and more threatening, and the public mind was rousing to perceive the danger and the necessity for resistance. The hospitality of the Berliners is proverbial, and I met daily in society not only Fichte and Müller, but Bartholdy and Humboldt. Humboldt had returned a year before from America, and Bartholdy had just arrived from Greece.

The season was delightful, and the city seemed at the culminating point of her prosperity before her great misfortune. It was a stirring time—the first dawn then appeared of a spirit which, though destined to be suppressed to all appearance by terrible events, was yet to rise again and free the people, and form a sure basis of regenerated prosperity.

The national enthusiasm was freely expressed in the circles where I visited: as a stranger I had been able to take a more general view of the relations between Germany and France, and though little accustomed to judge of diplomatic questions, I had understood enough to regard the state of things with increasing apprehension. As the danger therefore approached to Prussia I was far less hopeful than many of my friends, yet my fears then hardly assumed a distinct form. All that I valued most in Germany and on which the hopes rested which had tempted me to leave my native land, was despised by France and threatened with destruction. I abhorred the opinions she adopted, and her attempts to hinder the development of German thought and to obliterate German nationality.

This hatred I had sought in Halle neither to repress nor hide; on the contrary I had striven even in my lectures to excite a spirit of opposition to the baneful influence of France. The spirit which I tried to rouse had little reference to political relations; the resistance I then advocated was to be more inward than in act. Like German literature it was peculiar to no state; it was German, and not merely Prussian.

All that we heard in Berlin strengthened and confirmed our views; the spring weather was bright and mild; the chief persons of the city met at noon Unter den Linden, where the trees were just beginning to unfold their tender green, and all conversed upon the one great point of interest. When any remarkable excitement prevails, intercourse expands and is no longer bounded by the friendly circle, and I was thus led to converse freely with many whom I had but casually met before.

Prussia stood on the very brink of danger, Hanover was occupied by a Prussian army, and the Hanoverians hated the Prussians even worse than they did the French. A declaration war was expected from England—Russia threatened—Austria deserted by Prussia in her dangerous crisis was exasperate The state seemed doomed to be a prey to France. All that was noble and high-minded in Prussia appeared to be inseparably bound to England, and England was on the point of declaring war against her. Yet in that moment a spirit was engenderd which was destined to resist and conquer.

The privileges of the military were at that period excessive. Several instances came under my own observation in Halle to prove the truth of this opinion. The son of a merchant died in Malaga or Cadiz of the yellow fever, and his effects were sent home. The police were informed, the goods, chiefly clothing, were condemned to be burnt, and the merchant's house was placed in quarantine. Reil was loud in reprehension of the arbitrary measure, but it was not relaxed except in favour of a young officer who was engaged to marry the merchant's daughter and lived in the house; he was allowed free release from quarantine on account of the all-important parade.

Many examples also occurred of the overbearing pride of the military, and of their assumption that all honourable feeling were confined to their own order. These were venial faults compared to one which did not receive the censure it deserved. In 1805 there was a scarcity in Halle; public clamour was excited against a corn-dealer; his house was attacked, and the mob began to plunder a large stock of grain. The troops were called in, General R. himself was present, and the object being to protect the property of a citizen, I fully expected that he would have strictly performed the duty. I was amazed therefore when the general addressed the rioters as follows:—"My friends, I shall not prevent your helping yourselves as you please to the corn— take nothing else."

I was myself at last brought into personal collision with the military. Part of a large building, once the Jesuits' college, was appropriated to the natural history museum and lecture-room; on proceeding once to lecture, a student met me in great distress to say that he had been refused entrance by a sentinel, for the quadrangle in which the lecture-hall stood had been taken by the soldiers for an exercising ground. I appealed to an officer and was refused admission, and only after a very urgent remonstrance with the authorities did I receive a promise that similar usurpations should not recur. It may be supposed that my opinion of the military was not improved by this incident.

The summer passed while great anxiety prevailed in Halle, and yet no one seemed to forebode that our own district would be the seat of war. We all thought that a Prussian force would take up a position on the Rhine as in the former war. Most people relied on the effective state of the army; and under the supposition that the contest might issue in a defeat, it was thought still, that however grievous the calamity might be, it would not disturb our social interests. The fate of Austria did, not warn us of the danger, for the Prussians were accustomed to attribute far too great a superiority to their own troops above the Austrians. No one seemed to conceive the possibility that the University could be broken up; my classes had increased greatly in numbers, and for the first time I gave a course of philosophical experiments. Schleiermacher and my pupils encouraged me, and on the whole we were not much disturbed by approaching hostilities; on the contrary, our minds were rather spirited by the expectation of a crisis.

There were some who were at length overtaken by apprehension, and adopted a most unworthy mode of feeling and expression. Theirs was not real courage, springing from strength of mind, but a blind presumptuous belief in the invincibility of the army, which had been nurtured in untried times of peace. Such a spirit as that which nerved the English on the field of Agincourt would not have mistaken the danger. No one in Halle seemed at all to comprehend the might of a victorious army, whose commander had changed the whole tactics of war, and which, flushed by such victories as were before unknown in modern history, was now sent forth by the enthusiasm of the nation, and swept forward to destroy. It was imagined that the spectre of the Thirty Years' War would scare the enemy with mysterious horror, or that they would fly at the first sight of a Prussian parade.

The troops which had collected near Halle moved rapidly forwards, and reports strengthened of the advance of the enemy and of their having penetrated through Thuringia: at last the certainty that our neighbourhood would be the seat of war came to light. Many students had remained during the vacation, and many new ones had arrived, for the professors had not dared to quit the city. All remained for some days in anxious silence. Then the Duke of Wurtemburg entered Halle with his corps of reserve, and every inhabitant was seized with sudden dismay.

It is a strange, terrible idea to abandon oneself, helpless and unresisting, to a foreign power. As yet we believed ourselves protected by our army, but we were passive, and that firmness which springs from individual exertion failed us. I was passing through the streets with a Hanoverian *attaché*, who hated the French, when some troops of horse were moving on in disarray. "It is impossible," he said, "but that such troops of these must conquer; how truly grand is their appearance!" In fact, all minds were divided between an overweening confidence in the army and an irrepressible anxiety.

It became apparent, from the positions of the Prussian and French armies, that a great battle was to be expected. We listened breathlessly to rumours. At length the news reached us of the calamitous defeat at Saalfeld. It was whispered doubly at first, then more decidedly, and at last it was announced in the newspapers. Prince Louis had fallen. The daring with which the Prince had thrown himself on the enemy, and challenged an engagement, filled us with melancholy doubts and forebodings. Had he sought death in a desperate determination not to witness the subjugation of his country? Every new event feeds the imagination in portentous times; and the despair to which we attributed the destruction of Prince Louis and his host seized ourselves.

The disastrous 14th of October was near. The inhabitants wandered restlessly about the streets, for troops were posted in the immediate vicinity. Suddenly a rumour arose that a great battle had been fought on that very day, and that it was a complete overthrow. How the account could have reached us considering the distance of the field of battle, seemed quite inexplicable, for that there had been fighting near Auerstädt was already known. This gloomy report was soon after contradicted by more hopeful news. It was said we had gained a signal victory; the populace exulted, and even my immediate friends partook of the common joy. I still mistrusted; and feeling anxious for more certain information, ran at utmost speed on the road towards Merseburg.

About half-way the ground rises, and the Saltzstein Hill descends on one side precipitously towards the plain of Lauchstadt. I laid my ear to the ground, and heard plainly a distant cannonade. I distinguished that the sound rendered in a north-western direction, and became fainter by degrees: guessing the position of the forces, this appeared to indicate that the Prussians were retiring. I scarcely dared impart my fears to my nearest friends; but I remained uncheered by all the reports of victory, which continued strong even through the following day.

On that day a French prisoner was conducted through Halle; he was the first of the enemy that we had seen. How he came into this neighbourhood, whether as a straggler or captured in some skirmish, remained unknown; but his appearance caused a great ferment among the people. They surrounded him with screams and yells, and the soldiers who had charge of him had great trouble in protecting him against their violence. They seemed as if they thought in the person of this one prisoner to have won a great triumph over the enemy.

On the evening of the 15th of October I was told in confidence by the same Hanoverian *attaché* that a French division had fought its way towards Halle; and since I was fully convinced that the battle of Auerstädt had been completely lost, I now saw plainly that the reserve near Halle would be attacked.

My small dwelling into which I had removed from my first own spacious house was on the corner of the Parade, opposite the library. I looked from the windows over Moritzburg and Passendorf towards the hills which bound the horizon. In anticipation of a war I had often during the summer allowed my imagination to picture an army surmounting the distant hills and stretching out far into the plain: they had been my waking dreams, without any ground to justify the fancy.

Early on the 16th of October I thought I heard shots fired. I hastened to the window, and beyond the bridge which lead across the Saale to Passendorf I perceived in cloudy dimness a sort of movement which convinced me that a skirmish was taking place. The agitation, suspense, and dread of the last few days induced something like a tranquillized state of feeling at that moment when the danger assumed a more decided form. My wife had just weaned her infant; she was well and strong, and now that no doubt remained of the immediate presence of the enemy she seemed more curious than terrified. Schleiermacher came very early, with his sister and a friend named Gass, who was afterwards my colleague at the University of Breslau. He was chaplain to one division of the army, and waited for orders in Halle; they came to witness the military spectacle from our house.

We soon perceived that we should obtain a much better view by moving to the other side of the Parade towards the Freemasons' Garden, and we stationed ourselves upon a wall which was built on a steep rock overhanging the Saale, whence we commanded a sight of the whole plain; when we reached it many professors and officials were already assembled there; and a few parties of soldiers were moving over the long bridge. We witnessed attacks and interchange of firing, and saw dragoons unhorsed; but all seemed at first confused and undecided to our ignorant observation.

So strangely were most of the beholders blinded by the reports of victory, so confident were they in the indomitable power of a Prussian army, that in all these attacks on the French they were able to perceive nothing but evidence of our triumph. "Poor French!" said one; "I could almost pity them: it is clearly a body of stragglers, pursued and attacked in the rear by our victorious troops; if our bold reserve are upon them they will meet a dreadful fate."

Alas! we were not left long in our mistake. The enemy came on in larger masses; our troops fell back; we saw Prussians flying in terror even along the banks of the river close by our wall; and then everyone hastened in dismay towards his own dwelling; mine, in a remote, thinly inhabited quarter of the town, was considered both by myself and friends to be very much exposed; we hastily resolved to take refuge in Schleiermacher's, and hurried home to fetch our child. Gass led Schleiermacher's sister, Schleiermacher took my wife, and I followed with the nurse who carried the child. But we had lingered for too many precious moments at our home. We passed down the long street in greatest haste. Shots were fired in the town, and the streets through which we passed were still empty; every house was closed; in one place only I saw a workman tearing down hastily a tempting sign.

The nurse was herself a mother; she trembled, and though she tried to get on, she could scarcely hold the child; I threw its cloak over my shoulder, seized it, and hurried forwards. When we arrived where the street widens into a small square which opens on the market-place, we saw at once the danger which we had to meet. The Prussian reserve were retreating through the town; the centre of the market-place was filled with the cannon and ammunition of the fugitives, which a crowd of soldiers were trying to get away. We heard firing in the streets which led from the Saale and the market-place; and I saw that we must cross the stream of the flying mass at right angles. How we got through unhurt I cannot tell. In such moments thought is changed into a sort of blind instinct, and every power is concentrated in the immediate struggle for self-preservation.

We had crossed the market-place and were near the Mecker-street, where Schleiermacher lived. That street leads from the market-place at a corner which is common both to it and to the street, now the Leipzig-street, in which the pursuit was farthest. Once within sight of my street of refuge, I turned round to look for a moment; I was amazed to see the market-place empty; artillery and ammunition-waggons had vanished as if by magic, but the enemy were still pouring in thick masses from the streets which led from the Saale; a few Prussian soldiers were still flying hastily, and there was a general firing from the enemy in the direction of the retreat.

The balls whistled past my ears; I was but a few steps from the sheltering street, and yet for some moments I feared that I and the child should be cut off from it by the pursuing enemy. As we got under the protection of the houses we saw the little savage-looking men of Bernadotte's advanced guard (by-named "The Brimstone Corps.") rush close by us; but they were intent only on the flying Prussians. We reached the house; all was quiet in the street; the closed door was hastily opened for us, and for once we were saved.

But our repose was short, for the street lay too near the course of the pursuit: detached soldiers, both infantry and cavalry, were plundering in the neighbouring streets. The event had come so suddenly upon us, brought up as we had been in times of peace, that we knew not how to meet it or what to do. The street was narrow; some soldiers had penetrated in to the opposite house and were taking all they could lay hands on but they were plainly themselves in fear, for they made off when the people of the house called to us across the street. At last our door was knocked at: it was three or four horsemen who demanded entrance, but we took no notice.

They called out that they would be satisfied with a few glasses of wine given through the window. We determined foolishly to let them have it, though no one was willing to be the person to hand it over. I offered to do it, and the window was opened, but what you might have expected happened. A dragoon held a pistol to my head and threatened to shoot me if we did not unbar the door. We were obliged to do it, and the robbers rushed in. My watch was their first booty; I had no money in my pocket; some money and linen were hastily collected by Schleiermacher. On the desk among some papers lay the travelling money of the chaplain, Gass. They tossed about the papers, but, strange to say, missed seeing the money: we were then left undisturbed and had time to think of our position.

That the Prussian army was not only beaten but dispersed, appeared certain, and both town and university were for an infinite time in the power of the enemy. All our prospects were suddenly changed; the immediate danger was, however, too great to permit us to think much about the future.

The pursuit through the town was over, a few persons reappeared in the streets, not one of the enemy was to be seen, and in the afternoon I ventured as far as my own house to see what had happened there. I passed through some of the streets which led from the river; a few persons glided anxiously by, but went only to their nearest neighbours, and here and there a small group stood trembling and whispering together. There were rumours of fearful outrages committed in the suburbs, and the bodies of Prussian soldiers lay in the streets in their full uniforms; I saw one with his musket lying still by him. I found that the enemy had not been in my house, and I was able to collect my money and conceal or give into my friendly host's care everything of value.

We did not pass the night at Schleiermacher's; the bookseller, Schimmelpfennig, invited us all to his and we found many friends assembled there. Professor Hofbauer lived in the back part of the same house, and had heard nothing of what had taken place: we were obliged to call to him with loud voices that we were all in the enemy's power, and were witnesses of his horror. It is strange how a sudden, imminent danger changes the social relations of the inhabitants of a town. The subjugation of the country, the ruin of all that was sacred and dear to us, filled us with horrible imaginations; the intercourse of friendly families was suspended; we became familiar with whoever was nearest, for the next street, with the knowledge of its fate, was divided from us as if by an abyss.

Such of our party as had ventured beyond the house brought back fresh reports of outrages, so that the night was passed in dreadful apprehension—we expected burning, plunder, and violence every moment. We had assembled chiefly to protect the women, but our means of defence were small; we determined therefore to watch the night through; we knew that Hofbauer had a well-stocked cellar of Rhine wine, and we knew also that he was very chary of it, but by assuring him that what we did not use would fall to the share of the enemy, we persuaded him to produce a few bottles to support our spirits. We passed the night in a sort of desperation, and towards morning we all disposed ourselves on chairs and slept.

The night passed, however, quietly, and we found in the morning how groundless our fears had been. The plundering advanced guard had been obliged to follow up the pursuit, and had disappeared from the neighbourhood. The main body of Bernadotte's troops took possession of the town, and I must do justice to the discipline which they displayed.

CHAPTER 6

Napoleon in Halle
1806—1808

Bernadotte published the following proclamation in order to tranquillize the inhabitants.

AVERTISSEMENT.

*M. le Maréchal de Bernadotte, Prince de Ponte-Corvo, [-] de faire
connaître à l'Université de Halle, que le cours des [-] ne devait être
nullement interrompu; il a en même temps engagé tous les Professeurs
à continuer comme par le passé l'instruction des étudians, et il dispense les Professeurs de tout [-] militaire, &c. Ainsi les étudians qui se
trouveraient maintenant en route pour se rendre à Halle peuvent sans
crainte continuer leur route; M. le Maréchal a déclare qu'il etait dans
l'intention de son Souverain de protéger l'Université de Halle.*

*Malgre qu'il y a eu un combat très-meurtrier dans la ville, tout est
calme, et le moindre excès est réprimé.*

*M. le Maréchal s'est rendu en personne sur la place, pour commander
la plus sévère discipline, et a ordonné qu'on punît de [-] le militaire qui
ne respecterait pas la demeure des habitans.*

*Les fonds de l'Université resteront intacts, et il est défendu [-] toucher.
Halle, ce 19 Octobre, 1806.*

I hastened to post this proclamation on the door of my house. On
the succeeding days the anxiety continued to increase, a heavy cloud
seemed to hang over the city; troops kept passing through, and we
heard that Napoleon was coming, with the Imperial Guard. There
were reports that he was angry with the city, and still more so with
the university; in fact there was much to fear. Some of the students, in
desperate excitement, had even thought of asserting their independence against the French officers, and the professors were quite unequal

55

to keep them under safe restraint. I went with Schleiermacher to the Provost Maas to beg him to call a meeting of the council to devise necessary precautions; to our surprise we were told that such measures would be construed into acts of defiance against the French.

The provost, truly, was not very well calculated to bear an imposing front to the enemy; he was a little, miserable figure, he kept no servants, and it was said that the soldiers who were quartered on him made him clean their boots. Very few of the professors ventured out, and then only snatched a few hasty moments for conversation, whilst the students paraded the streets boldly in large and noisy parties.

Napoleon arrived. He took possession of Professor Meckel's house, in the Berlin-square, one of the largest in the place. The Imperial Guard made an imposing impression. Napoleon came on parade, and, it was said, made an animated address to those, his favourite troops. We knew that he was incensed against the Prussians. Halle was the first Prussian town which he had taken, and he had determined to remain there some time, while his troops pursued the routed army. I and my family were still in Schleiermacher's house, and the Secretary of the War department was quartered in it, who of course occupied the best rooms, so that we were all miserably crowded.

No one left the house at that time; no one had a comfortable bed; and we only snatched a little sleep when thoroughly worn out and exhausted. The Secretary who was quartered on us was polite, nay, even courteous. He often tried in a sinister way to engage us in conversation, and we therefore always expressed ourselves with great caution and reserve. One day he ventured to suggest to Schleiermacher that he should compose a letter which should attack the Prussian court and government, and speak of the hopes which the people of Halle cherished under the Emperor's protection. That such a man as Schleiermacher should have to defend himself from so vile an imputation enraged me much, but the official remained civil as before.

He once spoke without reserve of the Emperor's boundless ambition; he thought his views readied to the re-establishment of the Roman empire of the middle ages, whose beginning had been in France; that object once achieved, the Emperor, he thought, would grant a lasting peace, and foster the welfare of all his conquered subjects; the acknowledged civilization of the Great Nation would pervade all continental countries and help to cement their union, and no power would remain to oppose the conqueror or disturb the happy peace. Boundless exasperation, a hopeless sort of hatred, filled our minds whilst we listened to such detestable language, used by a German and in German words.

Napoleon remained three days in Halle: on the second he made a pompous procession through the streets, attended by his marshals and generals. He passed our house, and our official invited us to see the show. Schleiermacher and I refused, and after repeated requests would only throw a hasty glance or two towards the street, but it was not for long enough to distinguish the personages; I only saw Murat's rather fantastic costume; I never saw Napoleon. On the same day a student rushed into our room in boundless terror; I never saw hair really stand on end with fright before. Our minds were not in a state to admit of such a subduing passion—the more all outward help forsook us, the darker our fate impended, so much the firmer became our belief that the great and sacred principles which influenced Germany would survive to resist and to destroy our oppressors.

In this conviction I ventured to assert the strong opinion which I then adopted and maintained so long as the French kept possession of the land: even in those hopeless times I saw that the Battle of Jena was the first victory over Napoleon, for he then destroyed that weakness which was his best ally, and awoke in the bosom of every Prussian that spirit of resistance which was to fight and conquer.—The certainty that Napoleon would fall never left me.

The courage of the women in our fearful circumstances was remarkable, and though the excessive agitation of the young man led us to expect some astounding news, my wife checked the ebullition by exclaiming, "Fie! a strong-minded German youth should never look thus, least of all in such times as these!"

A deputation of the professors, headed by Niemeyer and Schmalz, had petitioned for and obtained an audience of the Emperor; they took Froriep with them, as best able to speak French. While the deputation was with the Emperor, a number of students had collected in the square. Schmalz, on their return, addressed the students, who, at the conclusion, gave some cheers, and it remained doubtful whether the acclamations were intended for applause or discontent. It had happened also that when Napoleon made his triumphal procession, some of the students had pressed carelessly towards him without bowing, and one whom he had spoken to had called him *Monsieur*.

Napoleon had, it was said, spoken severely against the inimical spirit of the university; such a temper, however strong it afterwards became, did not in fact then prevail. Napoleon might, perhaps, think that a large assembly of German youths of the best families might be, if not dangerous, at least inconvenient in the rear of his army. Unacquainted with the regulations of German universities, he fancied that the students lived in the several so-called colleges, and complained that they were not kept shut up in them. All this we knew before; and the terrified young student at length informed us that the university was closed by Napoleon's order, and the students were all to be sent to their homes: his great alarm was occasioned by an idea which prevailed, that when they left the city they would all be murdered on the road.

A great number of the enemy were quartered in the house where Schleiermacher lived. Towards morning we were awaked from our disturbed sleep by a great bustle in the house, continual running up and down stairs, loud talking, and the sound of horses' feet; the next morning the town was clear, the troops were gone. In the course of the day the students were all sent away; we, the teachers, remained behind in the waste, desert city, our office gone, our duty taken from us, our future all uncertain; only a few of the elder students ventured to remain.

All was at length quiet in the town; the professors assembled, and it was found that the funds of the university had been seized. Berthier had issued a notice from Dessau, in which the university was denounced as having deserved the Emperor's displeasure. Men of science, it stated, ought not to meddle with political affairs; their duties were solely to instruct; in Halle they had mistaken their position, and the Emperor had consequently determined to dissolve the university. Great as was our perplexity, I had believed that a body of German philosophers, though compelled by circumstances to submit, would have held a dignified line of conduct; but there were some who betrayed a cringing spirit—they proposed that we should disclaim all feeling of dislike to the Napoleon sway.

Such an assertion from me would have been false. I contended that we were not answerable to the enemy for any sentiments we might have entertained towards him before his occupation of the city; since that event we had been in his power, and we had done all we could to preserve order in the university. A servile address was, notwithstanding, sent to Berthier: for me to have published a protest against it would have been foolish temerity; but I was the more mortified because I felt convinced that the most slavish submission would not change the Emperor's determination.

Schleiermacher's position and mine were most distressing; our salaries were due in November, those of the previous months were spent. I had received about 80 *Louis d'ors* for entrance to the lectures which had been about to commence; I was thankful when the students left that this sum remained untouched, and when they were all repaid I had only 10 rix dollars left. Schleiermacher had about as much; there was no hope of help from distant friends, as the enemy possessed the country east and north. We determined to unite our scanty means, and live together in my own small house. My wife and child and Schleiermacher's sister occupied a little room; my friend and I shared another; and we had a sitting-room in common, where we both pursued our studies; in one corner of it he composed his treatise on St. Paul's Epistle to Timothy.

We lived on the poorest fare, seldom went out, and when our money failed I sold my plate. Yet, in the midst of all our privations, we did not lose our spirits; the firm belief that Germany would be redeemed through the unalterable spirit of the people supported us. Notwithstanding our poverty, we were able to collect the few students who had dared to remain, round our humble tea-table; it was fortunate that we had laid in a large stock of tea and sugar just before our misfortunes; there we saw Harscher, Müller, Von Marwitz, Von Varnhagen, and Blanc, the chaplain to the French congregation in Halle, who was our firm friend, and sympathised in all our feelings; those evenings will never be forgotten.

For the first few weeks we were agitated by continual reports of terrible events, especially by the sudden and, to us, inconceivable fall of Magdeburg. A number of Prussian officers, released from prison, returned to their quarters at Halle. Parade had formerly been held on the open square before our house; and when the town again became quiet, they returned to relieve guard at the old-accustomed place and hour. They seemed like spirits of the dead hovering about the treasure they had parted from.

Every scheme was tried by the enemy to prove the dispositions of the people. After a very few days' stay the French officers became tired, and required amusement; balls were therefore given, and all the ladies were invited, though the mode of invite was more like a command. I heard that some complied, but when we received our invitation we answered simply that our ladies would not attend. Many stayed away, but devised various excuses. I cannot describe the bitterness of our feelings when we saw these notes from persons calling themselves

Prussians, published in the newspapers.

Reil never failed to speak out daringly his honest sentiments; he often visited us, and came one day trembling with rage to tell us that the royal family had been attacked. I cannot say but that Napoleon's historical importance, at the time when he returned from Egypt, quelled the violence of the revolution, and restored order and prosperity to France, had excited a sort of admiration in me. I even looked with hope on the influence of his powerful genius over German development, but I despised him at last in the midst of his political grandeur. The greater his despotic power, the more sanguine did my hopes become; I believed firmly that I should live to see Napoleon's fall, and the country's liberation.

It must not be supposed that our scientific pursuits were abandoned. Our conversations all took a speculative turn; Blanc and Marwitz often took part in them, and there were evenings when the country's misfortunes and our own necessities were scarcely thought of. How dear my connexion with Schleiermacher became at such a time may well be conceived. At last communication was opened between Berlin on one side, and Copenhagen on the other; money was sent to us by distant friends, and our immediate distress was relieved. We had now to determine on our future steps; we wanted means of support and employment. Schleiermacher, with much self-denial, determined to I remain yet some time in Halle, where in seclusion he could complete with the least cost some publications he was engaged in. I had other plans.

My younger brother was with the troops which the Prince Regent had collected in Kiel, meaning to maintain an armed neutrality. He had represented my position to the Regent, who answered in the following words:—"Let him come back; he has a good head, and we can make him useful." I was greatly perplexed how to act: I was strongly attached to Prussia, I held an office from the government, and I did not acknowledge the power of the enemy to dissolve the university. Still my necessities forced on me the conviction that offers of employment in my native land ought not to be refused. I therefore wrote to the Minister von Massow, and stated that I still considered myself as professor in the university which had been destroyed by the enemy, but being without means of supporting my family any longer in Halle I craved permission to return to my native country.

This was granted me, and towards Christmas I parted from Schleiermacher and quitted Halle. On our route we were treated as fugitives with the utmost kindness. We stayed some days at Hildesheim, with my brother-in-law, Steltzer, and arrived in Hamburg about the beginning of the new year. There I heard of Blücher's bold advance on Lübeck—my enthusiasm, like that of every Prussian, on the sound of that glorious name was intense; it seemed a beacon of hope, and it was adored in Hamburg, where the greatest sympathy for Germany prevailed.

In March I left my family in Hamburg and went to Kiel. I found that the Holsteiners sympathized with Germany and could not endure the idea of the subjugation of Prussia, while the Danes, especially all about the coast, looked on with indifference.

I was presented to the Prince Regent; he received me graciously at first, but gave me to understand that I must not lecture. I ventured foolishly to remonstrate; he was displeased, and told me that I was bound to remain in Denmark and submit to Danish regulations. I replied that I then held an office under the Prussian government, and was only absent upon leave. His Royal Highness then spoke contemptuously of the Prussian army, and asked whether I meant to redeem the land by becoming a Prussian soldier. He was very angry when I left him, and as I passed through the ante-room I noticed that the attendants, who had plainly heard his loud angry voice, refrained from holding any communication with me.

I spent some anxious, useless months in Hamburg, and at the close of the year I was informed that the University of Halle would be reopened. Niemeyer had been taken as hostage to France, and, having been set at liberty, had visited Paris before his return; he had made some influential acquaintances there, and to them and his exertions the restoration of the university was owing. Napoleon's displeasure, and the strong temptation to the new King of Westphalia to advocate the final suppression, in order that he might seize the endowments for other purposes, made this act of grace difficult to obtain, so that great merit is due to Niemeyer's exertions in this cause.

As formal notice was sent me of the re-establishment of the university, with an order to return to my post, I determined to avail myself of the only apparent chance of providing for my family. My children's health not permitting a winter journey, I postponed my return till the spring lectures would re-commence, and in the meantime followed my friend Rumohr to Lübeck.

CHAPTER 7

Project to Murder Napoleon
1808—1811

The excitement which I always experience on revisiting old familiar scenes after long absence was never so great as on my return
to Halle. Though our journey was favoured by the most lovely spring
weather, my wife and I became more and more serious and anxious
as we approached nearer to the city. As the masses of buildings stood
out more clearly to our view, a deeper gloom seemed to overshadow
the place, and a portentous stillness reigned in it. The first few days
increased our comfortless impressions; we were like people who had
lost their all by fire, and who were come to seek for relics among the
ashes of their once luxurious home, but of ours scarcely a firebrand
remained; the place where our house still stood was scarcely to be recognised; the power of a destructive enemy had changed the outward
semblance and poisoned the inward springs of life.

Reichardt had fled from Halle with his family before the arrival
of the French, not having dared to await the vengeance of the Emperor, who had been incensed by a pamphlet written to undermine
his government. Reichardt was generally supposed to be the author,
and though it was never really known, it is probable that he at least
assisted in the publication. We found his house at Giedichtenstein in
ruinous desolation; Napoleon's persecution had ceased, and he was
living at Cassel as director of the opera, appointed by the Westphalian
government.

Schleiermacher had remained some time in our house and then
removed to Berlin: we found it just as he and his sister had left it, and
traces of his recent presence brought regret for his loss still closer
home to us. The remaining professors were almost strangers to me;
Reil, however, was still there, and Blanc: they were, in fact, the only
friends of former times remaining to us.

No session in any university ever opened so miserably; only three hundred students came up, not a fourth part of the former number. The lectures recommenced, and all went on formally as before; but the spirit, the intellectual aspirations which had before animated my labours, had faded under the oppressive influence of the times.

About the beginning of the second term it was determined to celebrate the revival of the university in ceremonious form. There had never been any edifice properly belonging to the institution, but an ancient house, containing some large, dismal looking rooms connected by long dark passages, had been hired from the city authorities. The ceremony took place there, and differed so little from all academic solemnities, with their long, tedious Latin orations, that I should hardly have recorded it but for a whim of the then rector, Niemeyer, to invest the whole proceeding with an air of antiquity.

Each faculty had to appear in the different robes and caps of the earlier period of the university. We looked like the spirits of our former selves—it was indeed a funeral pomp in its extremist sense, at which none but lifeless bodies assisted. The impression it made on me was revolting—I imagined myself surrounded by the infected atmosphere of a charnel house. It is not, however, to be inferred that among the professors all patriotic feeling was extinguished. The ceremony was very unwillingly attended, and perhaps no city in Westphalia contained truer adherents to the King in his adversity than Halle.

There were many ultra-Prussian patriots who accused Niemeyer of leaning too much towards the French interest, but he redeemed himself on many occasions from this suspicion, and when the news reached us of the death of our beloved Queen, his grief was excessive and most openly expressed. The despair which was felt by all in Halle at this event resembled that which followed the first subjugation of the city by the enemy—all mourned the loss with a feeling that the last weak hope had sunk with their beloved princess. Even the enemy seemed to respect this universal sorrow; but they little guessed the mighty will to resist and revenge which succeeded those tender regrets. The Queen's death was attributed to the unhappy position of the land. "The enemy has destroyed the protectress of the people" was the cry. She remained in death, as in life, the heroine of a struggle, the power to support which was strengthening by every succeeding event.

The new king, Jerome, honoured the University of Halle with a visit: he was attended by many generals and officials and by his counsellor of state, J. von Müller. I at first determined not to join the professors to wait upon him, but I was influenced to do so by a desire to see a man who had been raised from mediocrity, and after divorcing his wife in order to marry a German princess, had been placed by the despotic act of his brother upon a German throne. The whole body of professors and authorities of the city were assembled under Niemeyer at the entrance by which the King was to pass to his apartments. It was strewed with flowers, and young girls were stationed to receive him with complimentary verses. I felt as if this was a desecration of their innocence, and as if such honours ought never again to be paid to a lawful sovereign, for they had lost their value. Whilst we were crowded together waiting for Jerome many of the professors spoke out boldly against him. I was silent and overcome with shame at finding myself so placed, but my bitter disgust at the scene and at myself was not to be concealed.

There was a man named Rudiger amongst us, a professor of political economy; he was gigantic in height, and used to make himself conspicuous by many eccentricities. On this occasion he lifted his huge head and shoulders above the rest, and in his peculiar rough manner cried out, "Here we see the emblem of the city of Halle verified indeed." I asked what emblem he meant. "It is," said he, "an ass walking upon roses." This witticism was afterwards a subject of misunderstanding between Rudiger and me. Dangerous as such a remark was when uttered, the repetition of it afterwards found much favour in the victorious times of Prussian independence. He had, however, by that time forgotten having been the author of the sally, and was displeased that it was stated that he used it as referring to the arms of the city of Halle, whereas the ass on roses was only an emblem in use amongst the artisans: he considered such an inaccuracy, if attributed to him, a grievous slur on his reputation as professor of political economy.

The King arrived, but some time still elapsed before we were admitted. We kept modestly in the background while the under-prefect, followed by the clergy, stood close to the door ready to claim precedence. The doors at last were unclosed, and the prefect was ushered into the presence by an officer of state. Scarcely, however, had he advanced one step to begin his address when he was informed that it was the King's pleasure to receive the professors of science before the spiritual authorities, the precedence which had formerly been given to the clergy having been denied since the revolution. We were therefore introduced first.

The King stood in the centre of the circle; his personal appearance was mean; there was nothing manly in his features, which were disfigured by excesses; a stupid, hesitating manner betrayed the man, who had no innate power to distinguish him from the crowd. He made a short speech, assuring us of his attachment to science and his intention to uphold the university.

My days were passed in heavy, dull anxiety; there was but little emulation among the students, whose diminished numbers told fearfully on my contracted income. Even the few who remained belonged to so poor a class that few lecture fees could be expected. The Westphalian government also found pretexts to withhold a portion of our salaries, and by forced loans we were obliged to receive our payment in paper, which was not always negotiable. My studies, and a certain degree of danger which I knew to be the consequence of my avowed attachment, to the legitimate government, were the only exciting causes to keep me from helpless inanition.

I assisted in framing a proposal for a mining institution in Halle. The government at length partially adopted it, and named me as one of the directors, it being their policy to conciliate by such means those who were opposed to them; but I, determined to receive no income from them which I could not claim under my Prussian appointment—my only advantage derived from the institution was the means of extending the collection of mineralogy belonging to the university.

Halle, once the scene of brightest hopes, was changed into a school of heavy trial. I had lost my first child shortly after its birth in Copenhagen; the second, Anna, was born at Hamburg. She was a lovely child. My wife had lately given birth to a son. I was invited by my friends Blanc and Harthausen to join them in a geological excursion in the neighbourhood. Enchanting scenery, lovely weather, and friendly intercourse had revived our drooping spirits, but I felt an ominous depression when we approached the less cheerful district on our return to Halle.

We were not far from it when I saw a carriage coming towards us rapidly. I recognized a servant of our house; my heart sank within me. I seized the note he brought—my wife wrote in words barely legible—"Hasten home if you would see Anna alive."

I reached my house only in time to see my dead child. The sorrowing mother nursed her infant—it died three months after.

The death of my two children, the unceasing difficulty in supporting my wife and my remaining child, the restriction which cramped my usefulness in the university,—all pressed more heavily on me as the hope grew fainter of any change to mend our prospects.

Apprehension for my personal safety was at length added to the discomforts of a life of dejected inactivity. Professor Steinberg was shot in Marburg, so that I could not but perceive the possibility that a violent death might also be my fate: just at the same time Reil gave up all in Halle, and went to Berlin, so that my last supporter in the university abandoned me.

Napoleon mistook greatly the character of the German people. He had no conception of their attachment to their social condition under their own government; and while he calculated upon Prussian submission, he was ignorant of the indignation which was brooding over their violated treasures of hearth and altar, and of the strength which was growing up in secret for a final struggle. A venal press was at his service, but it hid the truth more from himself than others; and when that truth was spoken by a daring few, he wilfully misunderstood it. Napoleon hated men of science—"German philosophers," he said, "mix up politics even with their grammar and mathematics ;" but his act of tyranny in causing the bookseller Palen to be shot was a grievous error. He thought through terror to silence the reason of the country and subdue its spirit, and he raised against himself the fierce power of universal hate.

Had Napoleon pursued his advantage immediately after the invasion, there is no doubt that he might have annihilated Prussian independence altogether. The help of Austria and Russia, even if the former had forgiven the part taken by Prussia in 1805, would have arrived too late; but he spared because he little knew the power which was to spring up in the secret minds of the people. When it at length found a voice, he did not understand it. My pamphlet upon the universities was plainly understood by every German. Villars wrote to me upon it—

> You would have been lost if you had not written in a language which is as unintelligible as Sanscrit to the Frenchman.

A Frenchman would in fact have no idea that such effusions could have any political influence; yet I may venture to assert that it became the handbook to guide and rouse many of the German youth. This ignorance on the part of Napoleon and the French saved Prussia, and through Prussia, Germany.

A whole summer passed and no ray of hope appeared to cheer our darkness. The brave Spaniards fighting for existence were our only encouragement. Our own subjection seemed complete: Halle was the high road for the army, and every house was overrun by soldiers; Berthier, whose title of Duke of Neufchâtel brought painful associations, was in possession of the domain of Giedichtenstein, one of the most important in the kingdom. The King of Prussia was living in close retirement, first at Memel and then in Königsberg.

My first admission into the secret confederacy then forming in Germany was at a critical time, and it took place in a remarkable way. I received a request together with my friend Blanc to go to Dessau, and there at an inn I met many friends from Berlin—Schleiermacher, Reimer, Von Lützow, and others. Napoleon was then at Erfurt, surrounded by a circle consisting of the Emperor of Russia, the Kings of Bavaria, Saxony, Westphalia, and Würtemberg, the Grand Dukes of Baden and Würzburg, forty-two princes, twenty-six ministers of state, half a hundred generals, and—the actor Talma. The meeting, which was to conclude on the 14th of October, 1808, the second anniversary of the battle of Auerstädt, was devised, with the secret intention of promoting a project which was afterwards to change the political relations of all Europe, and Napoleon hoped to dazzle Russia by this ostentatious display of dependent sovereigns.

The object of our meeting at Dessau was not fully explained, but I learned that a number of confederates were distributed about the country to watch every movement of the French, and we were invited to co-operate and to choose discreet and faithful emissaries to assist us. I perceived at once that my friends were in possession of some unpleasant secret, and they afterwards confided to me that two persons had formed a plan to murder Napoleon at Erfurt. I need not add that the idea filled us all with grief and terror. That we should be freed from our tyrant by a crime, seemed to me the most dreadful of events.

I looked upon the mighty conqueror as a healing scourge sent by the Almighty in mercy; he was commissioned to strengthen the failing powers; to dispel the sickly apathy; to invigorate the loyalty, to warm the love of country; to give life and freedom to every dear and holy impulse; and if he were to fall by an act of cowardice and murder, all my brightest hopes would fall with him; even on the unlikely supposition that outward prosperity should follow, I should have lost the strong foundation on which I built my hopes of Germany's regeneration.

I waited in full confidence that the attempt would fail, and we soon found that I had not hoped in vain. Two men joined us in haste; their disguise was so overdone that I thought they could not have taken a more sure mode of making themselves objects of suspicion, and I was amazed that they had escaped the notice of the police. They told us that they had remained to the last at Erfurt, and had concealed themselves among the bushes when the review of the field of Auerstädt took place. Napoleon had actually come within pistol shot, but the Emperor Alexander had ridden by his side and sheltered him. The two conspirators soon left us, and I breathed more freely when they were fairly gone; we then separated, and each returned home.

Through Schleiermacher I heard of the state of feeling in Berlin, and of the good service to the cause which he and Fichte were doing there. The secret committee was to watch every movement in the French army, and obtain information of the feeling which prevailed in the provinces. They were to take advantage of circumstances as they might arise; and when Austria prepared for war, their time for activity began. Count Chasot was the president of the committee, and I received a letter from him, requesting me to assist him with advice and intelligence. Our difficulties were great, both to judge of whom among the lower classes we might confide in, and to find out how to keep up a safe communication with each other.

News reached me in 1809 of the intended Dörnberg insurrection, and of Schill's appearance on the Elbe. Many sober-minded persons were induced to believe that Prussia would be incited to take part in any bold effort. Scharnhorst and Gneisenau, though in the background, instigated the whole, and tried to influence the circle about the King, and even the King himself, to take a part; nothing, however, could be undertaken effectually without a general movement in the provinces.

These hopes of speedy liberation were blasted almost as rapidly as they had arisen. When the account of Schill's arrival on the Elbe was received at Halle the whole place was in great excitement. Many believed that the King, who still reigned in his people's hearts, would join with the Emperor of Austria, and that war would be declared. I was sustained by no such hope, though I believe that, had Prussia risen at that moment, a general confederation of the continental nations would have followed to support her.

A few days after I learnt how Dörnberg's effort had been crushed in the commencement; his secret had been betrayed, and he had nearly fallen into the hands of the enemy; this dispiriting news had already reached me when Schill's approach was announced. Proclamations were distributed, calling on the youth to join him. "You will," they said, "obtain no pay, but you will be honourably treated; all corporal punishment is abolished amongst us; we depend wholly on the noble spirit of the Germans."

When my young sister-in-law saw the paper she exclaimed, "Pay and discipline are not promised, but the people want and must have both." To my grief I am obliged to acknowledge that her keen remark was to some extent too true. When masses are excited to great movements, too much of the mean and pitiful in motive must always stand beside the high and great; other reasons, however, interfered to keep the people back. It was sad to see Schill's bold troop pass through the land, and not a man stand forth to join him.

An idea sometimes passed through my mind of the possibility of calling on the Halle students to rise with me and join Schill, and many of our secret confederacy hesitated with me. We all saw that from Prussia the new birth of Germany was first to spring; but Napoleon's success at Eckmühl, and his advance towards Vienna, extinguished all our rising hopes. The Westphalian government posted their boasting news at every corner of the streets, and the time for any hopeful movement had gone by.

A second favourable moment seemed to offer shortly after, on the occasion of Napoleon's reverse at Aspern; and, if both king and people had seized the instant for a general effort, who can say what success might have followed? But I have since reflected that, after all, it was a subject for rejoicing that the tempting opportunity was not improved. The vague elements of national independence were still too rude to be let loose, and a more fearful revolution might have followed and distracted Germany.

There were many painful stories current of the humiliating demeanour which Napoleon assumed towards the princes who had allied themselves with him. When I was in Hamburg I heard from Von Hammerstein, minister of the Duke of Oldenburg, an account of his waiting on Talleyrand at Warschau. He was sent to be the bearer of the Duke's resolve not to leave his own land and subjects. Talleyrand held soirees, at which he received the German princes, or their ministers in their absence. With his revolting, cold self-possession he used to take a prince or an ambassador by the hand, lead him into a window recess, grant him a quarter of an hour's audience, and then dismiss him and fetch another; in such an easy fashion was the fate of the small German states settled.

It was said that Napoleon was at the theatre at Carlsruhe when the old honoured sovereign of the state, the elder of the German princes, was in the opposite box; he had a habit of placing his hand in the breast of his coat. An adjutant was sent over to intimate that such an attitude was not to be permitted in the presence of the Emperor; the offending hand was slowly withdrawn. I shed tears of indignation when I heard of it.

Poverty began to prevail most fearfully in Halle; even the funds of the charitable institutions were exhausted; the salt-works—a great source of revenue—brought nothing in; and the inhabitants were plundered continually by the passage of the troops through the city. The University sank still lower, and the students still decreased in numbers. Vagabonds of all sorts passed in and filled the streets, and it was impossible to relieve the general distress; when it was tried to distinguish the number of paupers, and of those able to give relief, it was found that nearly the whole population were in a state of destitution. When this was ascertained, paralysing despair seized upon all; but it was with a suppressed rage that we perceived Napoleon waxing in his power, and heard of his Austrian marriage, and his extension of the French territory in Westphalia and Hamburg.

The University at Frankfort on the Oder had sunk almost to nothing, and in its place a new one was established in 1811 at Breslau, and I received with joy the offer of an appointment in it, with promise of an income sufficient to relieve me from all prudential hesitation. I accepted it at once.

CHAPTER 8

News of the French Disasters in Russia and of Napoleon's Flight

1811—1813

Whilst the university at Breslau was being formed, and while I continued to try to nurture to the best of my power those seeds of national independence which continued, in a cutting atmosphere, gradually, though by slow degrees, to fructify, the outward circumstances of the people grew darker and darker. Hard as was the outward tyranny of the invaders, their indirect influence was still more fearful and destructive. Nothing good could flourish under such a sway. In Breslau we heard much of the excesses during the war, and there were terrible recollections of outrages which had been committed by those troops of Southern Germany which had joined the French army.

Thus had German feelings under French influence been turned against their own country, and the fearful time seemed now approaching when a Prussian army might combine with the French for the final subjugation of the land. The heaviest oppression which I had witnessed in Halle seemed a light misfortune when compared to this. I foresaw that if the Prussians should learn to consider themselves as a part of the French army, and think it an honour to join them in the exultation of victory, the poison would be extended to the whole nation, and patriotism disappear wholly from the land.

I became acquainted with General von Grawert, then at Breslau, engaged in the topographical survey of Prussia, which was an important aid to my means of learning the form as well as structure of the Silesian mountains. His Adjutant-Major von Hiller, also became my friend. This truly patriotic-minded officer was painfully alive to his unhappy position, and his grief was extreme to find himself compelled to act against his country's interests. My conversations with him increased my own fears. It was clear that Austria must arm for Napoleon, now that he was son-in-law to the Austrian emperor; hence every hope was almost extinguished of resisting the subjugation of the whole of Germany. Yet I could not quite abandon hope; and our news from Russia of the determination after a lost battle to retire and lay the country waste revived it in the shape that the insanity of boundless ambition might there receive a check.

If the then state of Prussia was so overwhelming to me in my retired existence, how must those have felt who to the last had cherished a belief in the possibility of a general resistance! When the gloomy night of German despair was at the darkest, the secret league was still kept up, consisting of the noblest spirits both in Austria and Prussia, and they were connected by a secret confederacy with many among the German-minded English. Let the rulers who now sway the destinies of those three countries ever bear that league in mind, so powerless to all appearance then, and yet so mighty but a few years later: they will perceive in that time of cruellest oppression, that moment of impending destruction, and that rapidly succeeding liberation, a prophetic meaning for the guidance of future centuries.

Though occupied with the absorbing duties and interests of an infant institution, I continued to watch the political state of Prussia with passionate devotion. As the reports strengthened that Prussia, Austria, and other German states were likely to combine with France in hostilities against Russia, I longed to know whether such men as Gneisenau, Chasot, Eichhorn, and Schleiermacher had yet abandoned their last hope of freedom. Those few might yet withstand the withering influence which paralysed so many once undaunted patriots, an influence under which hope drooped and mutual confidence was changed into distrust.

Too many of the confederates, once secretly sworn to defend their country, strove amongst themselves, and a subdued people were armed to fight for the tyrant who oppressed them. But I felt that I had yet work to do. I could try to influence the minds of men and invigorate their failing spirits; and in the religious belief in a future but most certain triumph, I pursued the struggle, though unaided by the friends of more propitious times. At last I felt myself alone in the contest; I felt the pressing evils which bore down the boldest hearts as much as they did; but those very evils left no time for those around me to understand and value the great principles for which I strove. The sun of life seemed to have set, and midnight darkness threatened to overwhelm me.

In my deepest need I was suddenly supported in a most unlooked-for manner. In the last days of 1812 Gneisenau, Chasot, Justus Grüner, Moritz Arndt, and afterwards Blücher, appeared in Breslau. In the agitated state of the people these arrivals occasioned great astonishment. The police watched their motions, suspiciously, though without interference. I was brought into immediate connection for the first time with those men whose position and principles marked them as the hope of Germany. They passed much time in my house, when I took every precaution to exclude all other visitors.

Sometimes we met at a tavern, and remained in close conference till midnight; a small room behind the public saloon was reserved for us. It is easy to suppose that these arrivals in Breslau were the subject of intense interest, and that I appeared in a new character by my connection with them. The president of police said to me once that he knew that I had collected a little Coblentz, referring to the noble refugees who had made themselves extravagantly conspicuous in that place in the beginning of the revolution. I felt the remark to be a warning, but did not acknowledge the comparison.

This was my first personal acquaintance with Gneisenau. His I features were handsome, and his tranquil but firm demeanour bespoke the gentleman and the hero; his look was clear and open, and I never saw so happy a combination of self-respect and humility, of confidence and modesty. Like other distinguished German heroes, his views were formed more from observation than from books; but his regard for literary attainments in others was consequently still more to be admired. He never appeared to greater advantage than when he appealed for information on points where he was at fault, or frankly confessed any deficiency in knowledge. He had not the rapid apprehension, the sparkling wit, or the sarcastic vein which belonged to many commanders of the time, and which made them unpopular in society.

It seemed in the Prussian army as if the boldness which was 'ranked by military men as the highest of virtues was equally a merit in matters of the understanding, and the word of command was held as irresistible in controversy as at the head of a regiment. Many in maturer life had sought by force of natural acuteness to repair the deficiencies of early systematic culture. Others had attended the universities, but had suffered the military ardour of the period to break off their half-completed studies; an imperious tone on subjects which ought to be discussed with inquiring reserve prevailed especially in the unhappy year 1806. Those times had thrown back every strong mind upon its own resources. Never had men been called on to draw on their own powers to meet the exigencies of the time so as the Prussian officers were then. The effort led them on to victory, though it taught them overbearing manners.

I have had the happy lot to be in the society of many remarkable men, but I never regretted having a conversation interrupted as I have done when with Gneisenau; I never heard an unmeaning word from his lips; even on intellectual subjects there was, in his modestly expressed opinions, an irresistible weight; every ne felt the depth of his reflecting powers, and perceived that when he spoke, he thought more of that wherein he believed himself to fail than of the treasures of experience which he had gathered while assisting the greatest minds of the age to mature sound principles whereby to influence the fate of Europe.

There was something princely in his look and mode of expression; when his manner was most humble he seemed to bow with conscious self-possession; he was the most chivalrous, the most liberal hero, that I ever saw: whoever had the happy fortune to excite his interest might firmly depend on his effectual support under every circumstance. I think with gratitude of his benevolent goodness to me from the time that he first entered my dwelling; every remembrance of him is most mournful, but most dear. He came to me a few days before his sudden and deeply lamented death, with the dignified, firm carriage which he preserved even to old age. Never did the cholera seem to me such a cruel scourge as when it seized him for a victim.

Very different was Justus Grüner—a man who played an important part, but whose memory has been less recorded than that of military heroes: he was thin, and his fiery eye and pale cheek betrayed the struggle against passions in which he was not always victor. He had an immense quantity of hair, which was a fiery red, and he spoke with great ease and force: when he seemed most absorbed in conversation, he still observed most keenly, and he would fix his eye on someone and fathom rapidly how and when he might make him useful. As president of police in Berlin, he was able to do the cause good service.

Chasot was completely the officer: he had a robust frame and a superior mind; he had shot a French officer in a duel for having spoken with contempt of the Prussians. He lived to see no more than the dawn of recovered freedom, as he died while conducting the German legion on their return from Russia.

The powerful influence of Arndt's writings in Germany, in 1805 and 1806, is well known. Whilst other authors were awed to silence, he alone avowed his principles with intrepidity. His loud trumpet of war, which sounded its mighty alarm through the press, was not silenced through those unhappy years of tyranny. Calling for aid, it sounded on when hardly one sign of hopeful effort was apparent: he was destined to awake the sleepers—to arm the nation to resistance by words of strength and virtue. From the time we met he was my true friend.

That the state and prospects of Germany were the subjects of our continual discussions may easily be guessed; I then learnt that the secret league still existed in full force. We believed that we could trust England, though I must confess that neither the people nor their parliament seemed to afford that energetic sympathy with the oppressed continental powers which their position seemed to claim.

Austria seemed outwardly bound to France, but that this alliance would ultimately be more dangerous to her than the most unequal warfare, was as clearly understood in Vienna as in Berlin. The true-minded but timid Austrians, who feared a total overthrow in a contest with France, could not conceal from themselves that the treaty with her was a voluntary surrender of their liberties, while they could but seek an honourable fall by their resistance. Who has not learned from history that nations who have nerved themselves to the uttermost point of resistance, have found the germ of revived independence at the very time when its extinction seemed inevitable? while a yielding, timid people, like a hectic patient, fancies itself most secure when death is nearest, and, constantly deluded, resigns the last sickly hope only with the dying breath.

Everybody lived at that time in the intense excitement which prevails when a promise of being rescued from a wretched position has been observed, and the moment has not yet arrived for active exertion. The twenty-ninth bulletin had appeared: every artful expression in it seemed to endeavour vainly to conceal the news of a total defeat. The vision of a wonderful agitated future rose in every mind with all its hopes and terrors: it was breathed out at first in tones scarcely audible; even those who had believed that unbridled ambition would find its check in the land which it had desolated, could not realize the horrible destruction of a victorious army—an army which had for fifteen years, with growing might, excited first the admiration, then the terror, and lastly the paralysed dismay of all the continental nations, and which had at length been overtaken by a fearful judgement, more wonderful than its conquests.

But the strange event was there; reports no longer to be doubted crowded in upon us—the distant voice approached— the portentous words sounded clearer and clearer, and at last the loud call to rise was shouted through the land. Then did the flood of feeling burst from hearts where it had been long pent up—fuller and freer did it flow; then the long-hidden love to king and country flamed brightly out, and the dullest minds were animated by the wild enthusiasm. Everyone looked fur a tremendous crisis, but the moment was not yet come for action, and while resting in breathless expectation, thousands and thousands became every hour stronger still to meet it.

It was said that Napoleon, accompanied only by one of his generals, had fled in a sledge through Silesia, travelling day and night. A postmaster had recognized him in Hainau. In Breslau all was excitement, all household duties and affairs were forgotten, everybody was collected in the streets, and all looked for the leader who was to order them to arm.

The first thought was for the safety of the King: it was feared that, the remains of the French army might insure their safe retreat from Berlin by seizing his sacred person. Herr B. von L————, urged by this apprehension, addressed himself immediately to the King and entreated him to leave Berlin and repair to Breslau, where, on ground not invested by the enemy, surrounded by faithful subjects, he might be safer than in a city actually in possession of the French. Those who surrounded the King, however, feared his taking so dangerous a step. A few days after this Herr von L———— was seized in the night by *gendarmes*, carried off to Berlin and there imprisoned, though he was shortly afterwards liberated.

Though now at the very dawn of the long hoped for day, I felt myself strangely depressed. Six years, I said to myself, have I been looking for this moment as the most blessed of my life, and here am I, in a city remote from the scene of activity; farther south and west the liberators of Germany will assemble, and I must listen here inactively to accounts of stirring events as to so many tales. I was in this discontented state of mind when the report gained ground that B. von L————'s proposal was to be granted: it was followed by orders to prepare accommodation for the King and his suite.

And he arrived shortly after with his children. Hardenberg was with him, and a crowd of officers and generals followed. General v. York's intrepid action was soon reported, and the war was considered to have commenced, though no declaration had yet been issued; the influx of men, especially young ones, was enormous; every house was crammed, and the streets were all bustle. Scharnhorst had come—Gneisenau was expected—one feeling animated all; business, circumstances, connections, friendship, were thought of only to devote them all to the one great object, but that object had still to be viewed only through a mist of painful doubt.

The King had not approved of General v. York's open and brilliant demonstration; it was not impossible that he might be disgraced for it. The much-respected French ambassador, St. Marsan, accompanied the King to Breslau—the balance yet hung doubtfully, whether, notwithstanding the ardent longings of the whole nation General v. York might be sacrificed, and common cause made with Napoleon to attack Russia, or whether, allied with Russia, war should be declared against Napoleon.

Among those assembled in Breslau was Bolkenstern, who had been sent by Gneisenau to Halle to keep up the interest of our secret correspondence; he belonged to Scharnhorst's school, that is to the young officers from whom Gneisenau expected most in the approaching war. I joined a large group of officers at his lodgings, and learned that the *Gazette* of the same day would contain the King's appeal for a voluntary arming. All the youth of Prussia were expecting it, but on looking over a copy we saw there was no allusion to the object, and this paralyzing silence as to the enemy was discussed with great disapprobation and alarm.

In an excitement of mixed joy and apprehension I left the meeting. I passed a disturbed, dreamy night, and awoke early to prepare for a lecture on natural philosophy, which was to be given at eight. I had, as usual, not communicated to my family what had passed at Bolkenstern's, but an idea seized me—"It is for you," I said to myself, "to proclaim the war; your position permits it, and what the Court may afterwards determine will be indifferent to you."

I never doubted of the King's determination to join with Russia. That it was utterly impossible to appeal to the youth of Prussia to fight for France was perfectly clear, but there might be reasons for keeping the enemy in suspense, though after the King's appeal they were incomprehensible to me. It is possible, I argued, that to preserve this deception my open act may be disapproved, or even punished; I might be imprisoned—ruined. All this was unworthy of consideration at a moment of such urgency.

My class was not large, there was little interest in the university for philosophy, and the agitation of the time had thinned all the lecture rooms. I was just established in my new residence, of which the lecture-room and my study formed a wing. I was to give another lecture from eleven till twelve. The first was concluded, and no one had guessed what had occupied my whole mind throughout—it was that which I had for years striven for and longed for. I turned to my hearers and said,

"Gentlemen, I shall give another lecture at eleven o'clock, but I shall choose a theme of all-absorbing importance. The King's command for a general arming has appeared, or will do so today; I shall lecture upon that; let my intention be generally known. If the other lecture-rooms are deserted, it matters not; I expect as many as this room will hold."

The excitement in the town was unbounded, and the eagerness excessive to know in what direction the suddenly called out force was to be used. Thousands pouring into the town mixed with the inhabitants in the crowded streets, amidst troops, ammunition waggons, cannon, and loads of arms of every description. The slightest word calculated to throw any light on the state of things was caught up and repeated in every direction. Scarcely had the half of my two hours' interval elapsed before a dense crowd streamed towards my house, and the lecture-room was full to suffocation; many stood at the windows, in the corridor, and the crowd extended even far into the street, of those who could not gain admittance.

It was long before I could make my way to my place. I had not yet seen my wife that day; my father-in-law and his daughter lived a story above us, with Von Raumer; my mother-in-law was with us. The crowd which streamed towards our house amazed them, but I think they must have guessed at my intentions. My wife did not dare to venture forth, but I sent her a tranquillizing message by a servant, with a promise to explain all to her by and by. I had passed the two hours in great agitation: what I had to say—the burden which I had groaned under for five years—shook my whole soul; I was to be the first who was to cry aloud that the liberation of Germany, yes, of all Europe, was at hand.

I sought in vain to arrange my feelings into words, but I fancied that good spirits were whispering help to me, and I longed for the time of lonely suspense to be over. One thought came clearly to my mind—I reproached myself that I had murmured at being banished to a remote province, and now that very corner had become the splendid centre whence a new era was to emanate, and my voice was to set the elements in motion.

Tears gushed into my eyes. A short prayer tranquillized me, and I stood before the assembly. I know not what I said; had I been asked at the moment that I ended, I could not have told a word. I had no new cause to proclaim—what I said was but the echo of the thoughts and feelings of every hearer. That after calling on the youth to rise, I added my determination to take my part and join the ranks, may well be guessed without my telling it.

At the close of my speech I hastened to tranquillize my family; a few minutes after I was once more alone in my study. It is done at last, I thought, and a load was taken from my heart: but new cares now claimed my thoughts; from that hour my whole position in life was altered; arms were now my profession, and how was I to follow it? I had taken counsel with nobody, and I felt wholly at a loss. Suddenly a thought struck me, I would go to Scharnhorst—he would guide and help me best. I had taken my hat when a deputation from the students appeared: they begged me to continue my address in a larger hall, and named one which would contain five or six hundred hearers, and I was obliged to assent.

I longed to go, but could not get away, the students thronged in so continually. A precious hour had thus elapsed when Professor Augusti, then rector of the university, appeared; he had some important communication to make to me in private, and uneasy as I felt at the request, I was very glad of the excuse to clear my room of students. I was on the best of terms with Augusti. He said in a solemn way that he came from the Chancellor of State; that St. Marsan, the French ambassador, had hastened to the Chancellor directly on hearing of my address. He had inquired what it meant. "We are," said he, "at peace with you, and look upon you as our allies, and now a teacher in the university dares to declare war against us, as if under the sanction of the King."

Hardenberg had answered:

The feelings of the people, especially the youth of Prussia, can be no secret to you; we could not restrain the meeting—it was over before news of the intention reached us; the King discountenances it. Ask for an apology and it shall be given, but I cannot conceal that any step taken against the speaker would make him a martyr, and such excitement would follow as would make our position most difficult.

The Chancellor communicated to me through the rector that he had heard of my intention of resuming my address on the morrow. He did not desire me to refrain from expressing any of my own opinions, but entreated me not to mention Napoleon's name. By a sort of instinct I had avoided doing so in my first speech; I had feared that the name might give an air of personal hatred to my appeal, and rob it of the elevated tone of genuine patriotism. My friend left me, and I hastened to Scharnhorst. Colonel von Bayen, now minister of war, one of the most active and intelligent of our confederation, was already there. Scharnhorst embraced me, saying with joyful emotion—"Steffens, you do not know what you have done." I desired no greater praise; I foresaw that I, a quiet retired man of letters, in the middle age of life, would make but a sorry soldier, but that to the war I must proceed.

I had only lately become acquainted with Scharnhorst; he was not an officer of the Prussian parade style, but seemed more like a philosopher in uniform. He spoke like a man of deep thought, fully imbued with his subject, which was always one of real importance, and on which his deliberately expressed sentiments carried an irresistible conviction; both in argument and action he persevered in his point dispassionately, but with determination.

It is told of a legate who was sent to Paris by the Pope to transact business with Napoleon, that on one occasion he resisted the demands so obstinately as to make the Emperor almost despair of carrying his point. Napoleon at last left the room in high displeasure, and having ordered the legate to remain there till his return, shut him in and did not reappear till evening, by which time he hoped that weariness and hunger would have induced submission.

After a slight excuse from the Emperor, and a desire to resume the conference, the priest without a syllable of apology went straight forward with his business at the exact point at which it had been suspended. That was exactly the mode in which Scharnhorst always proceeded; he never flinched in anything he ever undertook against Napoleon, not even when success seemed almost hopeless.

Few were acquainted with the extent of Scharnhorst's powers. Invincible in purpose, untiring in action, all the wisest of our military leaders looked to him as the centre of their movements, To this great man I turned in the most exciting instant of my life for guidance. I told him that I wished to join one of the detachments of the regular army, and I rejoiced to find that he approved. "We can," he said, "place you at once at headquarters, where you may find work in which your former profession will be useful."

He advised me to learn the duties of the service, as at least in the beginning of the war it was desirable that I should be much among the young volunteers whose minds I had excited. He also advised me to present a petition to the King, praying to be allowed to join the service in whatever way His Majesty might please to appoint.

I was now perfectly at ease; my sudden impulse had become a well-considered line of conduct. I forwarded my petition, and in a few days received the following gracious answer:—

I afford you my entire approbation that you have not only excited the attendants on your lectures in the University to rise in their country's defence in the present imminent danger, but have also devoted yourself to the same praiseworthy service. To which laudable end I grant you leave of absence from your present duties until circumstances may permit you to return to them; and I heartily wish that the example which you have set to younger men, of devotion to their country's cause, may be followed to the happy furtherance of the same.

Frederick Wilhelm,

Breslau, February 16, 1813.

I passed the days which intervened before I received the royal answer in most anxious suspense. The lectures were discontinued, and I gave myself up to wild conjectures as to my future destination. I had not confided to my wife the important step which I had taken, and I had told no one but my father-in-law; who fully approved of all that I had done. I was beset with students in great numbers, not only of Breslau, but from Berlin, and in my state of uncertainty their eagerness increased my perplexity.

On the 20th of February I received His Majesty's letter permitting me to wear officer's uniform and act as an officer, until he should see fit to promote me to the rank of one.

I had now a distinct occupation. Captain von Bolkenstern, my sincere friend, commanded my company, and as a preliminary I paid a sergeant of the company to teach me my exercise, A rather laughable incident occurred in reference to my drilling. As every vacant space was required to exercise the volunteers as well as the regular recruits, the court of my house was sometimes used for the purpose. An old woman who worked occasionally in the family happened to see how the drilling officer sometimes lost his patience with awkward youths—how he seized the shoulders, pressed in the backs to expand the chests, poked the stomachs, and stuck a doubled fist under the chin to throw the head up. She had heard that I too was learning the exercise, and burst with loud wailings into my wife's presence, lamenting that I should have to undergo such treatment. My lot, however, was by no means so bad; my sergeant was very polite, though I cannot boast of being a handy recruit.

I could not, however, devote much time to these useful elements of my military education. I found endless and perplexing business in my office. A register had to be kept of every volunteer, specifying every personal particular. Many thousand volunteers came to me, and some generals who wanted volunteers to fill their detachments honoured me with visits. I had besides no little trouble with the young men, who all desired to join the guards, and who would with great difficulty be persuaded to belong to other corps.

A subject of dispute arose among those who had attached themselves to me. The young volunteers in other guard battalions had obtained permission to wear silver lace on the collar in the place of the white woollen which was worn by the regular men. The guard-chasseur company wore yellow lace, and the volunteers wished to be allowed to have it in gold. I must confess it was inconceivable to me how in such a moment of national enthusiasm the very weakest amongst the young men could think of such trifles; but Bolkenstern agreed with me in the propriety of decidedly refusing the pretension.

I looked upon it as one of the most useful circumstances of the times, that the more educated classes should mix with those beneath them in rank and cultivation. I hoped that the higher influence would gradually improve the whole army, and we determined that the volunteers of the *guard-chasseurs* should wear the woollen lace, and in all respects throughout the war be on an equality with the common soldier. The press for admission was so great that we did not fear to have our ranks unfilled: some of the most high-born among the youths supported our views, and many who have since filled exalted stations will remember the dispute, and how warmly they declared in favour of our determination.

The Lützow corps was being formed at the same time in Breslau, and I was excited to friendly emulation with Jahn, who was organizing his body of volunteers: his corps was most attractive to the youths of ardent disposition; the very spirit of chivalry seemed to expand amongst them—they were the poetry of the war, and their voice found noble utterance in Körner's lyre.

I had to manage for the clothing of the volunteers: the funds for the purpose were supplied by the voluntary subscriptions which poured in from all parts of Prussia. It is well known how boundless was the emulation to out vie each other in splendid contributions. The miser offered up his worshipped hoard; those who had not money sold their plate and jewels; and many an anxious mother was seen to fit out and send to the war the son whom she had scarcely trusted from her sight. Common and pitiful feelings such as will peep out to disfigure society in ordinary times then scarcely dared to show themselves; men high in station took their place beside the lowest; superiors seemed willing to receive commands from those below them, when they, by longer service, were thought more capable; the difference between giver and receiver seemed to have lost its former meaning; and truly those who witnessed such displays of national virtue after a whole century of peace-engendered imperious bullying, must have seen that which seemed either a miracle or a fairy tale.

To some of the poorer volunteers money had been given to provide their own outfits, and it happened sometimes that the small amount had been spent in drinking success to the common cause. I therefore determined henceforth to give nothing but uniforms and military accoutrements. Workmen were employed night and day, and the commander of our battalion, General von Jagow, proposed to me to equip with utmost speed fifty of the finest young men and present them to the King. The suggestion was complied with, though I would rather have avoided the display, in a wonderfully short time, and we received the royal permission to attend. The King received us in his palace.

Amongst the volunteers were the poet Burde and his three sons, all fine tall men, who stood far above all the rest. Burde had been secretary to Count von Haugwitz, and was not unknown to the King. The chief of the battalion alone was present; I was in civil costume, my uniform not being completed. The King received this first presentation of Prussian volunteers very graciously, and expressed himself to me in terms which I shall never forget: the audience was soon talked of, and as I did not return to my own house immediately, I found my door on my arrival there beset with carriages—it was men of consequence and generals, who came to congratulate me.

At length my transformation was to take place, and the process was by no means a pleasant one, bordering on the comic. The grave philosopher was to be changed into the raw second lieutenant. The little accomplishments which in youth are attained almost imperceptibly and are practised with ease were hard of attainment at my more advanced period of life: even the difference between my right hand and my left required reflection to remember, and the perception arrived always too late. I hoped that time and practice might remedy this deficiency, but it clung to me to the last—I began and I ended the clumsiest second lieutenant in the whole Prussian army.

Throughout all this preparation the alliance with Russia and the war with Napoleon were still undeclared. At length Baron von Stein arrived in Breslau with the news that Scharnhorst had met the Emperor Alexander at Kalish, and had there, on the 27th of February, concluded a treaty with Russia; but it was not until the 16th of March, almost six weeks after the royal command to take arms, that this treaty was communicated by Hardenberg to St. Marsan.

The Emperor Alexander's approaching arrival was announced, and the troops were ordered to line the streets for his reception. On this occasion I was on duty for the first time in my country's service. At four in the morning the detachment was paraded and marched to the suburb through which the Emperor was to enter. He was expected early in the morning; we waited in vain; the forenoon passed; we were all tired and hungry. Couriers brought news at last that the Emperor was still so distant that we might leave guard for half an hour. It was almost dark before lie arrived: he was received with acclamations by the inhabitants, but the enthusiasm would have been livelier had not everybody been worn out by hunger and impatient waiting: thus was I introduced to those minor duties of the service which are little calculated to excite or support the spirits.

War was declared in Paris through the ambassador. General v. York's demonstration was praised by the King, and became the universal theme of admiration. All the youth of Prussia were emulated by his example, when a most discouraging report arose. It was said that the enthusiastic love of liberty among the volunteer corps was disapproved in high quarters; it was considered extremely dangerous, and was to be restrained. They were not to act against Napoleon, but to be sent to Poland, where disturbances were expected, to protect the rear of the army. The exasperation may be conceived of young minds panting to be led against a hated foe, threatened, instead, to be used as a police force to coerce a people in whose cause they sympathized. Such intentions, however, if really formed, were not acted upon.

Our detachment was sent forward to Lissa. Bolkenstern and I were quartered in the fort, and my military life commenced. A grand review took place of the united corps of Blücher and Wittgenstein; it was my second public appearance as a Prussian officer. Bolkenstern worked very hard at teaching me to perform a salute. "When you are opposite the King," he said, "you must step forward with the—(I never can remember whether it was the right or the left)—foot and lower your sabre," and many more minute directions which I have forgotten.

They were my undoing; for when the moment came I was absorbed in thinking over my lesson, and my salute was so sad a bungle that Bolkenstern overwhelmed me with reproaches: happily I had no more such ceremonies to perform, for besides my inexpertness, my whole equipment was far from being a model of military perfection. The *guard-chasseur* uniform was very expensive, and consequently the gold epaulette did not grace my shoulder, nor was the *schako*, adorned with the black eagle, and the rich scarf, ever added.

The painful parting with my family had passed, and we moved on towards the enemy, who came to meet us with a rapidity which after so disastrous a defeat was truly admirable.—I must here introduce a few remarks to prepare the reader for the way in which I shall record my recollections of the campaigns of 1813, 1814. That which engrossed my mind throughout was a sense of the grand principle of the war, a conviction that it was not a struggle of the leaders, but of the people, nor waged merely to preserve a due balance of power—that balance had been long lost already.

Since the Thirty Years' War the influence of France had been but too predominant, and the later struggles, with the exception of those of Frederick II., had been mere phantoms of resistance. A nation bowed in spirit can reap but small advantage from a victory in the field, and brilliant as were the German successes during the last years of the reign of Louis XIV., and weak as France betrayed herself under Louis XV., she still maintained her sway over the whole of Europe. Germany lost her individual character in a servile and clumsy imitation of everything French; the most despicable adventurers cast out from France were at her courts, while French *friseurs*, dancers, menials of every description found a certain road to fortune by condescending to accept posts of honour among the barbarians of Germany.

In all history there is no example of such utter prostration of spirit, such voluntary humiliation, and not till all seemed prepared to extinguish the last dying embers of nationality was the spark of German independence rekindled. The war which followed was not one undertaken by a ruler and supported by his followers, but it was determined on in every honourable breast, and each man proclaimed it for himself. The moral question put to every mind was solemn—the answer was decided. It is true that a great part of Germany still remained attached to Napoleon—enticed, bound to France as in the unholy times of the Thirty Years' War, when Germans fought with Germans. But how remarkable was the difference between those times and these! Napoleon's great historical importance will consist in this, that by his open tyranny he destroyed the latent influence which had been growing-up for centuries, and by his violence forced every German to decide whether he would bow finally to the yoke or rouse to a saving effort.

During our tedious delay in Lissa, and our march through Silesia and the Lausitz towards Dresden, we were enlivened by meeting Tettenborn's division, advancing towards Hamburg, and Dörnberg's towards Lüneburg. I found Stein and Moritz Arndt in Dresden, where I remained a few days, relieved from the annoyances of military duty. It was my first personal introduction to the great German. I broke a lance with him, and my weapon was one which I knew better how to use than those which I had so lately assumed—it was a friendly strife, but an earnest one.

Stein was a man of deeds, not words, straightforward in action. He grasped and mastered every difficulty at the moment it arose, and he hated or pretended to hate speculation, and attacked me as a theorist. I was dining with him one day when only Moritz Arndt was present.— "Your propositions," said he, "are mere subtleties—bare *dogmas*, calculated only to cripple every enterprising deed."

"If," said I, "my speculations had not taken a practical turn, I should not have the honour to appear before you equipped as I now am; but the desire to realize all that is felt within, or apprehended by the senses, not according to outward semblance, but to the true spiritual import, is not the arbitrary whim of this person or of that, it is the moving spring of the mind of Germany, and through this it is that my friend Schelling has so influenced the national character."

"Yes," answered Stein, "I know well that the German youth are intoxicated with these vain theories; Germans have an unfortunate love for subtle reasoning, hence they neglect tangible good, and are the prey of every cunning enemy."

"Your Excellency," 'I said, "the German youth has risen in vast masses, yet many still hold back, and among those who do so I will venture to assert, not one of the intoxicated theorists is to be found. Who has more effectually incited the people to rouse and arm than our two great masters of speculative philosophy, Fichte and Schleiermacher? Your Excellency's time is too precious to be spent on subtleties which seem unpractical, but to me nothing seems more unpractical than to overlook a principle which you confess has become an element of the national mind."

I was almost frightened at my boldness. Stein grumbled rather angrily at first, but said smilingly afterwards—"Well, I am only an unpractical theorizer myself, wasting time in useless speculations on the views of others."

Mutual jealousies arose between the regular troops and the volunteers, whose unbridled ardour gave great offence. Many of those brought up in strict military discipline feared that the volunteer spirit would be a self-destructive element in the army, and held it their duty to keep it in continual check. Major von Z., who after Jagow's departure became chief of our battalion, had been General v. York's adjutant during the Russian campaign, and was highly esteemed by him. He was notwithstanding one of those who thought the volunteers ought to be kept under, and he expressed his conviction not only when I had the honour of being his guest, but openly before the whole detachment.

My unfortunate awkwardness, which was incomprehensible to him, called forth endless reflections upon useless, clumsy philosophers. On such occasions my position was not very flattering in the presence of my former disciples, among whom I was now the most stupid of the scholars; they supported me, however, on every occasion, and never failed to let me feel that they still remembered our former very different relation to each other.

Once in a village, the name of which has escaped my memory, a general advance was commanded. I was among the first who after a hasty equipment joined the major at the rendezvous, and was ordered to march with a small party in a certain direction before the village, in order to act as promptly as might be required on the approach of the enemy. I received no more particular orders. I ventured to inquire in which direction the enemy's approach might be expected.—"That you must find out," said the major, and I undertook the duty with much anxiety. I was utterly deficient in military experience, and was, as my friend Schall once called me in a poem, only a natural born soldier. I went with my small party in the appointed direction, judged as well as I could from very uncertain reports of the probable direction of the enemy, and posted two men on an eminence to reconnoitre, and behind them an advanced post—whether they were too far off or too near I was wholly ignorant.

The major came to review my position, and a storm then fell upon my unhappy head, which convinced me that I should not be able to continue that line of service. I was treated as the most incomparably stupid of human beings, the reproaches being varied by lively sallies on the uselessness of bookworms; in the course of these I was made answerable for all the trashy pamphlets of miserable authors which had been published since the subjugation of Prussia.—"Where did you look for the enemy?"

"There," I said, "answering to the reports."

"You should have expected them on the other side—you ought to have known better."

A large portion of the detachment were witness of this scene, including a number of my Breslau students. I had, as my rank required, received it all in silence, but later on the same day I waited on the major; he was more civil than before, and I sought neither to excuse myself nor complain of him, but represented that my position in regard to many in the detachment made it desirable for me to be appointed elsewhere, and that, as General Scharnhorst had only intended me to be in it for a time, my removal would save the major the unpleasant duty of correcting me in the presence of my own pupils.

It was then late in April, and we were approaching Altenburg, where General Blücher had his headquarters. With Bolkenstern's consent I joined them. Scharnhorst presented me to Blücher, who wished me to remain unattached, and all was arranged, even to my being provided with a horse, which Scharnhorst kindly undertook for me.

I found Gneisenau as commandant of headquarters, and Colonel von Müffling. The little town of Altenburg was in great excitement. The refugee King of Sweden, under the name of Colonel Gustavson, had lately arrived, and occasioned no small perplexity to the Prussian generals. It was very desirable to win over the then Crown Prince, Bernadotte, to join us, and it was plain that the exiled King hoped in secret to strengthen his own cause by the aid of Blücher and his generals, while he naturally expected that they would entertain no great partiality for the former French commander.

In the present important conjuncture, however, his absence was greatly to be desired, and that opinion was hardly concealed from him. I saw the thin, slender-looking King, one day, with his long, fair face, and the peculiar features of the ancient royal family strongly marked, standing at the door of a post-house; he wished to depart, and asked for horses, but all were under requisition. It was perhaps right to refuse them without orders, but a stable-boy did so in the most offensive manner, and I had the distress of seeing an anointed king, the descendant of Gustavus Vasa, and of that Gustavus Adolphus whose memory should be sacred in Germany, ill-treated by a menial. The King—for he had never ceased to be one in my eyes—made no reply; he turned away; and though his history inspired me with more pity than respect, I thought there was something truly royal in his demeanour. I was with Colonel von Gerlach: we both saluted him as he passed, and he received the compliment as a matter of course, and answered it with most kingly dignity.

Blücher was quartered at the Hotel Stadt Gotha. When I first joined the table there he was absent, with many of his officers. The Freemasons held a great meeting at Altenburg, and Blücher was the grandmaster. His love for speech-making made the society attractive to him, and it is said that he obtained his remarkable facility in speaking at the Freemasons' lodge. He came to the hotel before the dinner ended, and the conversation seemed to indicate that the war was about to begin in earnest, and that an engagement was expected. News was repeated that the enemy were advancing from various quarters. Councils of war were held, and I enjoyed the excitement of feeling myself in the very centre of important operations; my only perplexity was to wonder what sort of active service I could possibly perform.

One thing seemed certain—that I was to remain for the whole of the war at Blücher's headquarters. It is most difficult to give a true description of that wonderful man, whose memory will live as long as the records of the war itself; he has been so often sketched that it is hard for many to divest the personal idea of him of many trifles unworthy of his greatness. His *Life*, written by our great biographer, Varnhagen von Ense, is universally read, and deserves to be so.

Blücher might be called a phenomenon (*Incorrecte Erscheinung*); there was a want of keeping in the parts of his character, yet this very eccentricity produced his greatness. In him all that was strange and incompatible in that wonderful war was represented; therefore it was as easy for his admirers to throw all other heroes in comparison with him into the shade, as for his dispraisers to describe him as a mere phantom. The severe moralist will find much in him to censure, yet he was the very centre of the moral impulse of the war.

Compared with Napoleon, who invented a new system of military tactics, he cannot be called a great commander, yet in that character he won immortal fame. His speech was bold, like a rough, uncultivated soldier, yet sometimes it rose to such a pitch of eloquence as had been heard from no military hero of modern times; he obeyed the impulse of the moment, but the impulse was deep as it was quick; his perception was so vivid that he would see every difficulty in an instant and be dashed into despair; a few more instants and he would grasp the means of action, and fasten on his object with redoubled energy.

That object was Napoleon's downfall. His hatred to the tyrant mingled with the conviction that he was born to work his ruin, and he pursued his purpose as if led by an unerring instinct. He was a striking contrast to Napoleon: Napoleon studied all the phases of the revolution, and worked them out to the uses of his ambition, and he knew how to influence every ripple of the mighty stream which was to wash away the last traces of nationality. Blücher stood forth, a mighty nature, bearing the fire of youth in an aged but iron frame, destined to denounce the nothingness of the deepest scheming which was ever known in history.

The broken divisions of the beaten French army had to pass through a land inflamed with detestation, in order to join their reinforcements in their own territory. We must not deny the enemy full praise for the admirable tact and determination which they displayed under a calamity great enough to have over- powered an army of heroes. On their retreat a sort of preliminary war took place, which, compared with the great struggle in which all Europe was engaged, might be called an affair of outposts. The German legions, combined with the Russians, took advantage of the unfortunate position of the French retiring forces, and won successes which, at the time, were important.

Dörnberg's bold seizure of Lüneburg, and Tettenborn's occupation of the French city of Hamburg, were inspiriting incidents, raising the hopes of Germany, as did the first great overt act of General v. York at Königsberg. These triumphs had their value, but it was easy to perceive that the advantages could not be supported, and it is too well known how dearly they were paid for in both cities, especially in Hamburg; in the meantime the masses were collecting which were to decide the tremendous contest. France felt that she had to fight for her existence, and the magical word, "the glory of the Great Nation," was as yet in unbroken spell.

Napoleon was still to the French people their great leader, the conqueror of Europe, and the arming nations were rebels to his sway. Nature had for once joined to withstand him, and had triumphed for a moment; deprived of her aid, the resisting armies were again but the assemblage of so many easily to be re-conquered provinces. Holland, Belgium, Italy, and the south of Germany still obeyed Napoleon, and trembled at the power of his name; Westphalia was yet nominally French, though she was united in heart to us; while Austria, though wavering, was still in alliance with France. Many discouraging circumstances hung over the united enterprise of Russia and Prussia. A mighty impulse, it is true, had called up a Prussian army with a truly wonderful celerity, but the organisation was by no means complete, and time must elapse before any great force could be expected from Russia, distant as that country was, and exhausted by her late resistance.

This then was the state of Europe at the time when the new French army, issuing from their frontier, met the weakened forces returning from their Russian campaign: when a large division under General Wittgenstein, in conjunction with Blücher, prepared to meet the concentrated force of France.

In regard to my personal position I can only lament that I was as little qualified to be one of Blücher's staff as I had been for a second-lieutenant. I was devoid of technical knowledge, and though all were kind to me, each had too many duties of his own to find time to enlighten my unhappy state of ignorance; my records of the campaign will, therefore, be wholly deficient in military detail, and the reader will be less disappointed if he will permit me to call them, not a history of the war, but sketches of my adventures on the road to Paris during the campaigns of 1813 and 1814.

CHAPTER 9

Evening Before My First Battle
1813

Blücher had quitted Altenburg, and we all expected a general engagement. Late in the evening of the 1st of May I sat in lonely expectation in a small cottage. Though much excited by the prospect of a battle, my spirits were anything but elated, and I must confess that some personal considerations helped to keep them down. I had, it is true, been removed from a painful position, yet my present was unpleasantly dubious. Scharnhorst had not found time to give me any orders, and for the first time in my life I was without the power of independent action, and yet found myself in a moment of general preparation not only without any appointed duty to perform, but doubtful, were I to be employed, whether I should aid or impede the cause.

There was something cruelly humiliating in my situation, and the more enthusiastically I had anticipated the approaching contest, which had been the longing desire of so many years, the more wretched did I feel. I was pacing my little room with restless steps, when the sound of a galloping horse's feet stopped suddenly at my door. The rider threw himself off, and gave me a letter from Scharnhorst. "Here at last are my orders; now have I a place and part in the important day." I tore it open, and read as follows:

Dear Steffens,—I am sorry to be obliged to beg you to send me back the horse which I lent you. I lament that you will thus be prevented from appearing on the field of battle. It is the animal which I always ride on great occasions; and I fear that you will be obliged to remain in the rear to await, as I trust, the victorious issue of the day.

I gave up the horse, and now I was in despair. If I were absent from the field I felt that I should be disgraced, and incapable of service for the rest of the campaign. I had heard the name of the village where the *garde-chasseur* battalion was posted; I set off and by walking a mile joined it at last, though, having had some difficulty in finding a guide, it was nearly morning before I reached it. I called up the chief of the battalion, and begged him to put me in the way of obtaining a horse. I was conducted to a countryman, who at first stoutly resisted my demand, but at length produced one. It was a yellow chesnut, old, half-starved cart-horse; his ribs might be counted, and his hips stood up like the sharp sides of a rock.

I climbed up to the miserable saddle, evidently the peasant's own manufacture, and after much effort the poor animal got its limbs set in motion. It was obstinate, and its mouth was as hard as iron. No Prussian horseman ever cut so strange a figure. The knapsack which the guide had carried was fastened behind, and it was long before I got the clumsy beast into a trot. Which way to look for the field of battle I knew not; but as the day began to dawn I thought I perceived troops in the distance, though I was quite ignorant whether they were friend or foe. I rode forward, however, till I reached a large, open, gradually sloping field.

Here I found a large body of Prussian infantry formed into line. How it took place I cannot tell, but suddenly I found my horse and myself in the very front, hindering the advance. An officer of rank, who must have been greatly astonished at the singular apparition, came up with angry looks, exclaiming, "What the d—— are you doing here?" General von York had been pointed out to me in Altenburg; I recognised him with dismay, while I made a desperate but for some time unavailing effort to induce my charger to retire from his position.

I have but a confused impression of how I got out of the scrape; I only remember the sound of the General's scornful reproof .When I subsequently became well acquainted with him, and related the history of the disaster, he was highly entertained. After many inquiries and much riding backwards and forwards, I found Scharnhorst. He told me to remain near him, and ordered one, of his adjutants to mount me on a baggage-horse. It was nearly noon, and the engagement began; but I had no idea whatever of the position either of our force or the enemy's. Cannonading was heard all round, and the enemy seemed to be behind Gross-Görschen, but I could not perceive them.

I rode together with Gneisenau and the officers surrounding Blücher. The enemy stood before the houses of the village. A charge of cavalry was made on our side, and I suddenly found myself in the midst of a shower of balls. Prince Wilhelm's horse was shot dead under him. The charge was repulsed. Of how I got into the midst of it and how I got out again I can give no account whatever; only two things remained clear on my recollection: one was the sensation caused by the enemy's grape-shot.

It seemed to me as if the balls came in thick masses on every side—as if I was in a heavy shower of rain without getting wet. Yet I cannot say that I was exactly overcome with fear; the impression was more strange and peculiar than alarming. The second object which distinctly impressed me was Prince William. He was then about thirty years of age, handsome in person, with the undaunted air which belonged to his royal race; and he was mounted on a splendid charger, which he managed perfectly. As he rode, smiling and composed, amidst the shower of balls, he seemed to me like a fair vision which I shall never forget. Gneisenau seemed quite joyfully in his element. Immediately after the attack he gave me a message to General Wittgenstein, and now began my darker part of the day.

I rode forward, and looked about. That the battle was still raging near Gross-Görschen was proved by the tremendous cannonade of the enemy. I had no idea where to find Wittgenstein. Everything round me seemed confused, and as if I was covered with a veil. I felt a tottering, a swimming, which sprang from my inmost soul, and increased every moment. I was plainly seized with a panic—the cannon fever. I found Wittgenstein notwithstanding, and delivered my message; and as I returned I met the detachment of my own volunteers, who as yet had taken no part in the engagement, but expected orders every instant to advance. I described to them under all the excitement of the moment exactly what I had seen and experienced. The young men listened with thirsting curiosity.

It is well known how they distinguished themselves that day by their daring valour. When I rejoined Gneisenau all was in active engagement, every man knowing his duty and working hard in his appointed place. Nobody of course troubled themselves about me, and the feeling of my inability overwhelmed me, whilst I was obliged to stand there a mere useless looker-on. I perceived Scharnhorst carried wounded away; I had lost sight of Gneisenau. I was surrounded by strangers, and I found myself at last alone, with the enemy's balls howling around me.

There are several sorts of courage as well as reasons for its failure. I was on the battlefield for the first time, not only without any distinct duty, but contrary to the orders of my commanding officer. To the consciousness of this I attribute the uncontrollable panic which seized me, yet I never entertained an idea of retiring from the scene; such a possibility did not once occur to me, and I managed to collect my senses so as to observe what passed for the space of two hours. Sometimes the fight in and about Gross-Görschen came nearer to me, and I saw the Prussian cavalry exposed to the fire from the guns. I saw how their ranks thinned, and how, as here one and there another was unhorsed, with frightful wounds, the rest quietly closed up and filled the spaces.

At length I found myself late in the evening again with Gneisenau, and close to the village. He, who must have noticed my agitation, was himself perfectly calm and cheerful, notwithstanding that the issue of the day was still uncertain. "Steffens," said he, turning to me, "is not that a grand cannonade? it is to celebrate your birthday." He had passed the last anniversary with me in my house; that he should remember and joke upon it at such a moment struck me as wonderful. As it became dark I joined Major von Schutz at a bivouac fire, and there heard of the advance of our cavalry, which attempted a charge against the enemy. That charge failed; and although we maintained possession of the field from which the enemy had withdrawn, it was determined that we should retire towards Pegau.

I rode in the dark by the side of Schutz to the edge of a rather steep declivity by which our troops were marching in slow and perfect order, while other detachments were reposing by the bivouac fires, which lighted up the trees. The impression of such a scene, which afterwards became familiar to me, was at first very striking. We reached the little town in the middle of the night; it was crammed with troops, but we got a tolerable lodging, and through intelligent officers who had been in the engagement I got some general insight into the events of the day and their results. This was most welcome; for hitherto all was mystery and confusion to my understanding. The object of the great contest, as it had engrossed me for so long, again rose clearly to my perception, and I felt convinced that I should not meet a second battle as I had done the first.

In spite of our retreat we looked on the affair as a success, for the troops had stood bravely against Napoleon, and a most valiant spirit pervaded the whole army. Satisfied with our position, and reconciled with myself, I slept.

On the 3rd of May I joined Blücher in Borna, and found the troops in regular march, all in close order, as if going to meet an enemy; nothing betrayed the appearance of a retreat. Blücher had received a slight wound, but was in high spirits. Prince William was with him, and remembered that he had seen me early in the fight, and I received compliments which were far from being due to me, and which made me feel ashamed, though I trusted and believed that, had I been in the performance of some active duty, I should have found my courage much more manageable than it had been in my idle position.

For the first days the retreat was continued over a sandy level. Blücher was in the midst of the troops as they proceeded leisurely. The army was in such perfect order that many considered the retreat an unnecessary disgrace, and as this opinion was rather boldly expressed, it came to Blücher's ears, who thought it necessary to address the troops about it. This was my first opportunity of admiring his astonishing eloquence. The substance of the speech is generally known, for it was published to appease the whole army, as well as to tranquillize the people.

"You are right," I heard him say, "you are not beaten—you kept the field, and the enemy withdrew; their loss was greater than yours;" and he then explained to them all his motives for not pushing on the battle, as well as those for retiring. I heard him repeat the same to various divisions as they came up; and while I praise the facility and noble simplicity of his expression, as well as the power of giving the same meaning in so many various forms, as often as he had to repeat it, I must confess that there was something besides the words which gave such effect to the address, and that much was owing to the appearance and manner of the aged but powerful-looking man.

We were not attacked that evening, though the enemy followed closely on our rear; a few unimportant skirmishes only took place; nor was our actual retreat much molested till we reached Meissen. I remember once at Müldethal, where the army had to cross the river, there was considerable confusion; the valley widened at the point of crossing, and was surrounded by rather high hills. Just as the confusion was the greatest, news arrived that the Russian General Milaradowitsch was fiercely attacked.

While I looked anxiously about I perceived that Blücher and his followers were as calm possible, and that no movement took place, except that adjutants hastened backwards and forwards from him to the Russian general. It appeared to me that the heavy firing both of cannon and small arms was approaching fast, and I fancied every minute that the whole hostile army would burst upon us. I felt like a landsman in his first storm at sea, who looks with amazement at the composure of the sailors. Milaradowitsch, however, withstood the attack, and soon came up with Blücher, without any considerable loss.

When we halted on this side of the Elbe, near Meissen, the two armies were posted just out of reach of gun-shot, but the outposts, who were stationed on each bank of the river, opposite each other, frequently exchanged shots. We stood on a height out of the reach of the fire, but near enough to observe how men in each party quietly levelled their pieces, and took deliberate aim at individuals, and when a man fell we heard the shouts of joy. I have felt firm while I have seen many fall in battle, but this savage coolness filled me with horror.

We still retreated slowly. Blücher's headquarters were at a village behind Bautzen, and he remained there some days while continual skirmishes took place. The King and royal family were lodged in a castle close by, and I had the honour of being invited to dinner by Prince Augustus, who had sometimes talked with me during the retreat. Prince William was in the same castle, and they both had a separate dinner at the same table, each for his own guests. Through Prince William's adjutant I obtained the luxury of a bed, which I had not enjoyed for many nights, and I had scarcely thrown myself into it half undressed, when I fell into a sleep so sound that it lasted far into the following day.

We passed our time at headquarters very idly and wearily; at length it was varied by the arrival of some generals, who held a council of war. We lingered before the house trying to catch reports, but could learn nothing positively, though it was generally understood that we were to take up a position and offer battle. Many jokes passed upon this movement, and it was asked whether it was to be made in fact, or in a Fichtian sense— in a positive or a transcendental mode. There seemed no expectation of a real, important conflict.

Many of the ultra-patriotic had proposed that the Southern Germans, who were taken in arms against their country, should be shot. It was thought that it might have a useful influence on those German troops which were in the French army, and that they might in consequence come over to our side. Of the probable reprisals very few seemed to care, or of the bitter spirit which would be infused into the war. Some of the Würtemberg prisoners were brought to our village: I was by Gneisenau when he addressed one of them, a very fine-looking young man; he tried to make him perceive how wrong it was for Germans be fighting against their countrymen. The man looked good-natured, but stupid, and was evidently a fresh recruit. "I would rather have remained at home," he said; "father, mother and sister cried when I was taken away, but I was obliged to go, though I did it with a heavy heart."

"I should like to know," said I, as we walked away, "whether any German could be so fanatic as to shoot such a poor wretch as that."

"Not yet," answered Gneisenau; "but if, from which God keep us this war should last for years, who can say what we may do. The blood of the men of the Thirty Years' War runs in our veins and after long-repeated provocation and mutual barbarities, we may become such as to afford our enemies a sure and bitter triumph, even should we conquer them."

Early in the morning of the 20th of May I received orders to summon Lieut.-Colonel von Witzleben from his post behind Kleinwelke, the Herrnhuter colony. The landlord of the Hernhuter hotel told me that he saw plainly that their town would be within the scene of battle, but he displayed the most perfect composure. The whole town wore its usual friendly and tranquil aspect, very few people were in the streets, all was in order, and all quite quiet in the hotel, as was usual among the Herrnhuters. When I had delivered my despatches to Colonel Witzleben, he informed me as a warning that the enemy was close at hand. I was uncertain which way to go. It was plain that Blücher was concentrating his force, and I hardly hoped to find him again in the village where I left him.

It was a lovely May morning. I rode forwards uncertain whether I should pursue the road or turn back, and I soon perceived the glittering of arms before me. Some horsemen here and there rode out singly: I recognized the enemy, and found myself pursued. As I galloped swiftly back again through Kleinwelke, I saw the sisters in procession in their simple, exquisitely neat costume, passing quietly on to the church; I could not pause, the enemy were close behind, but I carried with me a vision of peace and heavenly piety, displayed for one moment on the spot where human strife and slaughter were so soon to rage.

I reached some Prussian troops, and was directed by them to the heights of Krickwitz, where I should find Blücher. It was near noon. As I rode towards him, over an inclining plain, I saw many skirmishes around, and got into the midst of a hot fire from the enemy. Whether the impression caused by the pious sisterhood supported me, or whether use was beginning to blunt my sense of danger, I cannot tell;

but freely as I confessed my panic on the field of Görschen, so must I now be allowed to say that no idea of fear at this time came into my head. Some rising ground prevented my seeing the heights beyond, and while I saw other officers dashing hurriedly across the dangerous field I was able to turn with composure to inquire my way. I found that our troops were all in the hollows, and when I perceived that I must pass over the rising ground before me, which was fully exposed to the fire, I felt it almost entertaining that I should be the only poor mark for the heavy cannonade.

I found Blücher. The hill which he occupied, and on which he was closely surrounded by his staff, is strongly impressed upon my memory, for we kept our post there the whole of that am the following day. A bare rock of granite crowned the hill and it commanded an extensive view, including the widespread field of battle. To our left lay Löbau—exactly before us Bautzen; the town was obscured by intervening hills, but its towers were to be seen above them. The Spree flowed on the right, the banks strongly defended by our troops; and beyond perceived Kleinwelke, which I had so lately left, and which, as a point of sacred interest, attracted my eye and feelings during the whole course of the two days' battle.

Every part of the field was clearly visible in the bright dazzling noonday. We saw the Russians fighting near Löbau. The scene of the hottest fight was between Bautzen and us, on the banks of the Spree; it was partly hidden from us by the hills which rose on each side of the river, but we could hear that the firing was very sharp and heavy. Some cannon-balls came amongst us, and scouts were continually coming and going, had brought with me a very excellent mounted Dollond from Breslau, which was in great request among the generals; where it was at liberty for me to observe particular parts of the field, my attention was riveted to the spots where great struggles were maintained: especially towards Löbau where the Russians were engaged. I saw first one and then another fall, and the contending masses advancing or falling back from either side.

When I lifted up my eyes for a general view, what a strange scene it was! The district was fertile, the villages numerous—all, as we supposed deserted by the inhabitants. The whole country seemed to have changed its character; a tragic veil hung over every object by a fatal destiny lowered over every town and hamlet. In 1817 I again passed over the battle plain, and saw the fair landscape and the peaceful villages; but the fearful picture of it as I had beheld it disfigured by the war, rose to my memory, and seemed to hide the happier present from my view.

It became dark, the firing ceased all around, and a wonderful repose succeeded to the turmoil of the day of noise and strife. Only here and there a single shot broke on the stillness of the evening. On the whole the issue of the first day was satisfactory; our troops had nowhere been beaten from their positions, and our head quarters remained on the same heights throughout the night, since it was determined to renew the contest on the following day. I stood, late at night, by General Braun, of the Artillery, and we counted the blaze of eighteen burning villages; my heart bled for the poor inhabitants.

The soldier is sadly too soon absorbed in his own work; the most humane learns to think of the inhabitants of the theatre of war as being only so much inconvenient encumbrance which must be got out of the way; but the mass of soldiery let loose their wild and destructive passions to oppress them. As I gazed on the burning landscape fearful images possessed my imagination; women with their children, in despair—men who would protect them—butchered; maidens flying from ruthless pursuers; a host of spectres surrounded me and filled me with an overwhelming terror.

Such terrible sensations did not again make me their prey; they were the result of our singular position. The Krickwitz Heights were almost in the centre of the military operations, and it was necessary to defend them at any cost; the enemy were therefore kept as far as possible off in a vast semicircle; and those who were not sent with orders to different parts of the field had time to observe and reflect, while the mind fed on its own resources to lay up fearful images for the hours of repose.

We were, as it may be supposed, careful not to attract the observation of the enemy by any bivouac fires. I wrapped myself at last in my cloak, laid myself on the grass, and got a few hours' sound sleep under the mild May sky. The cold air of the morning waked me, as well as the companion who had slept by me; he was the son of General Scharnhorst, and had been one of my former pupils in Halle.

The early rising thus in the open field, at the dawn of a fresh spring morning, produced a very different impression from that felt on a morning before an expected battle, when the night has been passed within quarters. Everyone sleeps then, as it were, within reach of his arms; but on rising, usual habits are not neglected—preparations for the day, for dressing, and breakfasting, are even more carefully attended to than usual, and the contrast is striking between the little cares incident to common life and the great events which the day has to disclose. Here, as we awaked in the midst of the open landscape, Nature herself in her power and grandeur filled the mind with lively emotion.

Young Scharnhorst was not without good hope of the issue of the day which was dawning upon us. He had received a slight wound from a shot which grazed the ear, which, though not severe enough to disable him, caused him considerable pain. As we sat together a peasant family approached, a man with wife and child; they had lingered after all others had fled in a village which was in the centre of the scene of contest, and their terror was great. We knew not how to advise them; but as they had been long without food, we shared our breakfast with them.

Scharnhorst explained minutely the position of the forces, and pointed out clearly how all ours had entirely maintained their posts of the preceding day. Everything as yet was perfectly still; but in less than another half hour shots were heard here and there as the outposts skirmished with each other. A heavy gun from either army sounded a solemn morning salute, and generals and adjutants were again grouped together. The attack became rapidly more general; soon it was hot everywhere, and it was the same vast struggle of yesterday, suspended only by the few short hours of darkness. I saw how fierce the fight was towards Löbau, and from thence in our direction, and what great exertions we had to make the whole morning to maintain our ground.

The enemy's cannonade was directed towards the central hill where we were posted; it came every minute nearer, and sounded heavier; the villages through which the retreat must be made, in ease we should be compelled to retire, were in imminent danger; yet the road was still open to us behind, and the enemy pressed on in front harder and harder. It was nearly noon, as far as I remember, when no hope remained of our being longer able to maintain the Krickwitz heights. I shall never forget Blücher's rage when he called furiously for his horse, intending to lead on a charge of cavalry. The generals, however, surrounded him with entreaties to abstain from so desperate a measure, which would risk everything by sacrificing his own life. They restrained the veteran with the utmost difficulty, and a general retreat was ordered.

We moved towards the town of Buschwitz but little molested by the enemy, and our head quarters rested there some time. I was near Prince William, and had another opportunity of seeing him escape from an imminent danger. A cannon-ball struck the ground just under his horse; the horse, of course, plunged forward, and the ball rebounded high upwards in an arch, without injuring anyone in the dense crowd amongst which it fell.

We continued the retreat through Reichenbach and Gorlitz, and reached the Silesian frontier at Waldau. Many skirmishes took place, and some attacks from the enemy, which were so repulsed that the order of our retreat was not interfered with. It was in one of those that Duroc lost his life by a cannon-ball, as he was riding by the side of Napoleon. We saw the confusion which ensued, and guessed that some great personage had been wounded. Since the beginning of the battle of Bautzen we had had little refreshment; a retreat is always a time of privation. Waldau is a considerable town, with a large trade in Bohemian and Hungarian wine.

I turned into a wine-house, where the cellar-doors were pressed on by a crowd of soldiers and officers mixed together. I reached one at last, bought some wine which I gave to a soldier who waited on me, and retired to the refreshment-room to enjoy some of it with a few companions. I had sat there quietly for some time, when I discovered that I had lost my purse, the contents of which were considerable and my whole resource for the greater part of the campaign. I rushed out in dismay, entreated the crowd before the cellar-door to make way for me, and found my purse where it had lain undisturbed for half an hour; *Cossacks*, Russians, and Prussians had come in crowds and gone again, and not one had discovered the treasure which lay at his feet.

I had another adventure in this place. I was quartered in one of the remotest houses, and being very tired, slept most soundly. At the first break of morning a loud knocking at my door roused me. "Come instantly!" cried a voice; "the place is evacuated, the enemy close upon it; we have only this moment remembered you in your distant quarters." I was of course dressed in a few minutes, and soon mounted; I hastened towards the castle of the village, the road to which I knew. I found it deserted both by inhabitants and soldiers. General Krauseneck alone still remained; I found him in an empty room, and learned that a *Cossack* detachment had abandoned their outpost by mistake, thinking it protected by the Prussians. We got up with Blücher only at some distance from Waldau, on the road to Haynau.

I obtained information that the retreat was to be continued beyond

Schweidnitz, and a stand was to be made there in order to conjoin with the newly-organised Prussians and the advancing Russian troops. Breslau was to be abandoned. At Halle I had felt once what it was to know that my family was in the enemy's power, and I had determined, if I were to join the army, that they must be placed well in the rear.

I easily obtained leave from Gneisenau to go for a few days to Breslau, and thus, I grieve to say, I lost being present at the brilliant affair at Haynau. That unpremeditated and successful attack, as well as the conduct of our army during the retreat, assisted greatly to convince Napoleon of the serious prospect of his campaign. The French pursued us with so little precaution, as our spies informed us, that they were in a state to be overcome by any sudden attack. It was said that Major Rühle often pressed Barclay de Tolly to take advantage of this opportunity; and it was not until the absence of that general that the advice was acted upon, and followed by a brilliant success.

CHAPTER 10

Attached to the Russian Corps
1813

Prince Bishop Hohenlohe-Bartenstein had offered his residence at Johannisberg as a place of refuge to Councillor Schultz and his family, and my wife accompanied them thither. I left Breslau after two days' stay, and rejoined headquarters in Reichenbach. Berlin was threatened as well as Breslau, and the old men, women, and children hastened towards the Austrian frontier; all the young men were with the army.

Fresh Prussian troops were continually arriving, Russians marched into Silesia from Poland, and every street was full when I reached Reichenbach. The whole allied army were grouped round that centre. The Emperor of Russia and the King of Prussia were near, first in Schweidnitz, and afterwards in Obergrödizberg; Moreau was expected. An alliance had been formed with the Crown Prince of Sweden, but great anxiety was caused by the truce which had been proposed by Napoleon before the battle of Bautzen. It was feared that he would use the time to influence the Austrian court, and there were fears that many even in the Russian and Prussian courts were still secretly attached to his interest.

There were rumours of a proposal from Napoleon, that the Elbe should be the boundary of his territory. At Blücher's headquarters the determination was fixed and strong, that he should be treated with only on the other side of the Rhine. The two battles which had been fought rather raised than depressed the hope of future victories; and it was loudly proclaimed that the war must be carried forward in the spirit which gave rise to it, and that it would remain a deep national disgrace if it were abandoned without a signal triumph, such as should cripple Napoleon's power for ever. I was too much behind the scenes not to be aware of the doubtful and dangerous point on which our deepest interests turned.

We were reduced at last to rest our hopes on one man, and that was Napoleon himself: our chief reliance was on his obstinacy, which might exhaust the patience of the negotiating princes. The truce was declared on the 5th of May, but the war was apparently suspended only to be secretly pursued by our enemy by means of different but more dangerous tactics; and the better informed among us knew that the secret weapons of the foe were now used in the very midst of us. Two months passed on with the daily anxious inquiry, "Will Napoleon win Austria, or will Austria be true to us?" The news of Scharnhorst's death, which took place in Prague, was an inauspicious omen, and increased the painful doubts of that most anxious period.

During the truce I was employed to collect secret information regarding the enemy. Von Oppen furnished me with a correct statement of the French forces and their positions, from the Bohemian frontier on their south as far northwards as the Elbe. My duty was to ascertain, by all possible means, every movement and change of position, and to report continually to headquarters. It required much activity and promptness in the use of the various means placed at my disposal to acquire information, and great care to sift and verify that which I succeeded in arriving at.

I travelled a great deal in the course of this mission, and remained some time both in Altwasser, near Waldenburg, and also at Schmiedeberg. After some experience the work became exceedingly interesting, and during the whole war I was never engaged so fully to my self-satisfaction. My sense of the small amount of service which I was able to render in the field will, perhaps, incline the reader to be patient while I congratulate myself on this one occasion. The occupation of Lähn was a strong reason with Blücher to determine on breaking the as yet unexpired truce; and I may venture to believe, that my communication on the fact conduced to the adoption of that measure, which proved so important for the success of the campaign.

I received orders to join General Pahlen, who commanded the advanced guard under St. Priest, and to continue my communications as before. It was expected that the enemy would advance upon Schmiedeberg, and in order to be near the General, I took up my quarters at Ober-Schmiedeberg. The town stretches itself, like most in mountainous districts, to a great length; so that, at first sight of the handsome buildings which present themselves on the road from

Hirschberg, the traveller expects to find a place of much importance. Farther on, however, as the valley narrows, it loses all pretensions to be more than a poor village of the hill country.

I remained for the night in an old, dark, and long uninhabited country house; the spacious suites of gloomy, neglected apartments had a ghost-like appearance, and I and my servant were the only occupants of the dismal mansion. When I rose the next morning in order to seek for General Pahlen, I learnt that our troops were again ordered to advance, and I rode eagerly towards Hirschberg, curious to witness the first meeting of the Russians with the enemy.

In Hirschberg, however, I obtained no information of the progress of the troops; but advices reached me from headquarters stating that General Pahlen had been sent on other service, and I was ordered to join his successor, General Bistram. I proceeded, therefore, towards Greifenberg.

As I approached Greifenberg I heard a sharp firing of small arms and a few heavy guns. General Freissinet was endeavouring to defend the town, in order to cover his retreat; the position of the place was favourable to him. The river runs close to the town, and the houses rise one above the other to some distance up the bank. A cross fire, very harassing to the Russians, was opened upon the bridge. I had no clear idea of such a fierce attack, and thinking to find the General in the midst of the fight, I rode to the bridge, and found myself in the midst of the fire. I there learnt that he was at a village at some distance, and of course, retired to seek him, but not till I was convinced that the enemy would be able to maintain the town at least till late in the night.

I must be permitted here to introduce to the reader a personage who may be thought hardly worthy of a page in the history of the war, though, in the sketches of my personal adventures, he ought not to be silently passed over. This was my servant, a youth of about sixteen, whom his mother had confided to my care, trusting that I would protect him from the worst dangers of the war. I had lost sight of him during the retreat, and he did not rejoin me till the middle of the truce, by which time I had felt very uneasy on his account. I was attached to the lad, though he had shown no very soldier-like qualifications, and it was plain that he had preferred to remain behind while his master had had to struggle both against the enemy and his own sensations.

He had passed his time with other servants in the rear, and it seemed that they had fed their imaginations with marvellous stories of the deeds which graced the front, and had become, at length, inspired to emulate their masters, every one of whom was more or less a hero in their eyes. As he, at length, rode after me upon the bridge of Greifenberg, and heard the balls for the first time whistling around him, his exultation was extreme. He reproached me for leaving the bridge—"This is as we ought to be; why not stay?"

The meek boy was suddenly transformed into a warrior. On one other occasion I also observed his usual disposition suddenly reversed by circumstances. When I was gathering intelligence in the Lausitz, we arrived, after a lonely ride, at a country house which had only just been quitted by the enemy; the inhabitants had deserted it before. The doors and gates were all wide open, windows were broken in, and the court in ruins; inside the house, shutters were torn from the windows, the mirrors cracked, the carpets in shreds, lying with the remains of broken furniture in wild confusion. My poor servant was usually not only gentle and obedient, but honest, and for his age remarkably careful of the property of others.

The traces of plunder, and the sight of so much destruction, seemed, however, to revolutionize his character in an instant. His eyes gloated with desire on the wreck of valuables as he rushed from room to room, seeking for some treasure which might have escaped the spoilers' notice. But the plunderer's penetration had been sharp; the lad sought long without success, while I looked at him in silent astonishment at the sad but rapid change. I at length spoke some admonitory words, and having reawakened his slumbering integrity, and obtained a promise to resist future temptations of the sort, I allowed him to retain a pair of leather gloves for the winter's use.

A suddenly heated imagination, on such occasions, aids to throw the sense of rectitude off the balance: at other times my poor lad's fancy was as tame as any uncultivated peasant's could be, but I doubt not that visions of rich treasures buried under ruins, or purses of gold forgotten by the flying inhabitants, rose in irresistible power to tempt him from his usual habits. In the war of liberation much care was taken to prevent plunder; it was, however, never wholly repressed. This may be attributed to the hasty organisation of the army, which precluded all sufficient training or strict discipline. The nightly bivouac, in the absence of tents, also hardened the feelings of the men. An encampment admits of some of the regulations of a social condition, while the bivouac fire encourages the licence of a brigand.

I found General Bistram; he was a well-educated Livonian, who, when he had received my credentials, treated me very courteously. He gave me an account of the engagement at Katzbach, which increased my regret at having been absent from our headquarters at the time, since the attack differed materially from those which I had witnessed. It was undertaken in a tremendous storm of rain in the midst of a stream from the overflow of the river. As the muskets would not go off, the ancient feats of personal prowess seemed called again into action; bayonets converted muskets into lances, and the engagement became individual, in which the bodily strength of our men had a decided advantage. Friends and foes were mixed in fearful entanglement, but the enemies were pressed into the stream, and the success was complete, the general of division Puthod being finally cut off from the main body.

By this affair and by the battle at Gross-Beeren our campaign was re-opened under circumstances highly animating to the troops. The army moved forward, pursuing the enemy through the Lausitz towards Dresden; they made a retrograde movement after the unfortunate engagement near Dresden, but when that temporary reverse was so brilliantly recovered at Culm they again pressed forward. When we were posted near Seidenberg on the second advance I thought it desirable to attach myself to the *Cossacks*, and at my request two hundred were placed at my disposal, and an officer who knew German was appointed as interpreter; he commanded the troop, I only decided on the destination.

On the first appearance of the *Cossacks* they were regarded as objects of terror, but they were not on the whole very dangerous enemies, and they often individually displayed much gentle good nature. We always approached the enemy very cautiously, and I sometimes slept at one extremity of a straggling village whilst the enemy occupied the other; I reposed on the instinctive sagacity of my escort. Sometimes when we mustered to proceed after a night so passed we found prisoners amongst us, though I could not tell how they had been captured.

One reconnoitre which I made with the *Cossacks* remains fresh on my memory. The enemy had retired behind the Neisse and had taken possession of Gorlitz. I rode along the side of the river on some heights which ran parallel with the banks, and from whence I had a clear view of the French position. The inhabitants had learned during the truce to know the different corps and distinguish the officers, so that I obtained some valuable information from them. As I rode on I perceived on the opposite side a gay summer encampment; it was a number of fanciful *arbours* formed into regular streets; some of the bowers had vestibules or porches decorated with wreaths or twined with flowers; they were not yet faded, and their appearance was most lively.

Some of these flowery tents were larger and stood apart from the rest, and as I afterwards entered them I found they were divided into chambers, and had plainly been the summer houses of the commanding officers; they were surrounded by little gardens divided into beds, and many a pretty flower was still in its perfection of bloom; so that though deserted there was no trace of decay or confusion. It was impossible not to admire the light-hearted people who thought it worthwhile to embellish the scene of their brief rest in the midst of a hard and uncertain life.

After a time General Bistram was ordered on other duty, and General B—— commanded the advanced post, with which I remained. I was much struck with the great number of general officers among the Russians, whereas there were but few officers of distinction in the Prussian army. Langeron was the commander-in-chief of the left wing of the Silesian army, and St. Priest commanded the advanced guard under him. The small corps to which I was attached consisted only of about a thousand men. I was often at St. Priest's table, and there was a much larger assemblage of generals than at Blücher's headquarters.

The number of orders and high-sounding titles were not less remarkable than the excellence of the table. Blücher's was very frugal, or only well supplied when we remained in larger towns, but the Russian owed his luxuries both to the care of the officers and to the singular adroitness of the *Cossacks*; their talent for foraging exceeded that of the Prussians. At General B.'s I was sure to find choice fish and game.

I once proceeded with my troop after a reconnoitring expedition to Radmeritz, where St. Priest was quartered. There is a convent there for young ladies of noble families. It was nearly evening when I arrived, and as I went to seek the general I observed a number of officers in full uniform stepping from stone to stone up the dirty road which led to the castle. I found that the general gave a ball, as it was the custom to do on every possible occasion, both with the French and Russians, little regard being had to the small amount of pleasure which the poor ladies might be able to take in the festivity.

My interview was scarcely over with the general when Blücher appeared in Radmeritz and took up his quarters in the convent. It was a great joy to me to see him again, to be once more among my friends, and learn their adventures since we parted. The ball went on and I had to be an actor in a provoking scene: a folding-door opened, and the venerable old abbess followed by some of the young ladies who did not dance appeared in procession, and advanced straight up to me; the abbess greeted me with an address which threw me into the greatest confusion. Blücher was present, and as much astonished as I was at the demonstration.

A young man then advanced, whom I did not know in the least, and introduced himself as Count von Löbau, known as a poet under the name of Isidorus Orientalis, a disciple of the new school, especially of Novalis. He was son of the abbess, and during these critical times he was living in the convent as guide and protector to the ladies. He had thought it his duty to celebrate the arrival of a brother philosopher and poet under such unusual circumstances; and for that purpose had got up the ceremony, not troubling himself about the figure which I might cut in the eyes of my military friends. Blücher looked displeased—the other officers amazed; but they were civil to the ladies, and wished me joy on the honours heaped upon me, which were the least comfortable that any man ever enjoyed. I had to bear them all, as well as an abundance of ridicule.

Having received orders to rejoin Blücher's headquarters, which were again at Bautzen, I proceeded thither and found the place almost as tranquil as in times of peace. The comparatively small number of troops were bivouacked in the outskirts, and the usual business of the inhabitants was little interfered with. My feelings on entering the town, now quietly in our possession, were very different from those with which I had gazed on its towers from the Krickwitz Heights on those two days of fierce contention. I remember as I passed along the streets that I envied every neatly-dressed civilian whom I met; his position was properly my own, and I was in disguise in my irksome uniform.

Three Silesian militiamen were now placed at my orders, and remained with me till our approach to Paris; they were to act as couriers when I should be distant from headquarters. They were willing, but not very efficient; the *Cossacks* were far more useful, and understood the slightest sign better than the Silesians did the clearest orders.

During our stay in Bautzen important negotiations were progress between the Silesian and the main armies. I almost always dined with

Gneisenau, together with many officers of the staff. One day he was in great spirits; the conversation turned on the victories we had already won at Dennewitz, Jüterbogk, and Culm; at length Gneisenau said, with the most confident air, "Gentlemen, we shall taste this year's grapes on the Rhine do not mistake me, I mean the last grapes which, in November will yet be hanging on the vines."

I guessed that this decided belief must spring from some great intended enterprise, of the success of which he felt assured. Yet Napoleon was still mighty he ruled not only over France, but great part of Germany, Italy, Belgium, and the Netherlands; and though his fortunes seemed critical in Spain, his resources were enormous. Gneisenau's positive prediction was therefore startling.

Blücher's army crossed the Elbe above Wittenberg: it was early in a fresh, clear October morning. For many hours the infantry kept continually passing in close and rapid order along the floating-bridge, then the cavalry crossed over, slower and more carefully. The arms glanced in the sunbeams, and old legends sprang up in my memory, while first the reflection of their bright weapons, and then host after host, was seen coming from afar, till every hill blazed with glittering life. The enemy were hidden behind the great wood of oaks which borders on the river; a few cannon-balls reached the Elbe, and some which struck the surface of the water rebounded and sprang in wide arches upwards.

The whole was a most lively spectacle: we feasted long upon it, for Blücher and his staff did not cross the river till a considerable part of the army had reached the opposite shore. The enemy, divided from us as they were by the wood, had misdirected their fire, and as long as I stayed to witness the passage not a shot reached the bridge. As the troops landed, they disappeared again behind the wood. Our headquarters remained some little time in the wood, but Blücher soon disappeared with some of his adjutants, and I and others were ordered to remain there and wait for him. I was with my friend Von Raumer, who had joined the army during the truce, and whom I had met with much joy in Bautzen; we were now near to his native town, and we knew that a great battle was being fought. I am able to give but little account of it. We heard the heavy firing, and the cannon-balls broke great branches from the trees, which crackled and fell all round us; but of the fight we could distinguish nothing.

Now and then indistinct rumours of the fate of the battle reached us, and we heard in particular how bravely the Silesian militia had stormed the heights which surround the castle of Wartenburg. At last we received orders to advance, and we reached Blücher just as the victory was won and the enemy retiring; only a few skirmishes with General Bertrand's flying corps were still kept up. Blücher took possession of the castle. We were shown, with a number of officers of the staff, into a great hall, where the walls and floor were torn and injured by the cannon-balls: one ball had been reflected from the floor, and had passed quite through the wall. Preparations were made for a feast of rejoicing, and we all assembled.

The day had been a glorious one, but as yet we could hardly reckon the results. The Crown Prince of Sweden had now to cross the Elbe with his troops; the great body must advance strenuously and take up a concentrated position, so as to challenge the enemy in every direction, and compel him to a decisive engagement. Now I perceived what had so inspirited Gneisenau at Bautzen. The movement from Bautzen to Wartenburg had been so accomplished as to deceive the enemy. Divisions had approached the river at various parts, making demonstrations of attempts to cross at all of them, while the plan had been laid for a sudden passage and an immediate attack by surprise on General Bertrand's force. It was General v. York's corps which gained this victory: his resolute conduct decided the event of the day, and won the honourable appellation which is now borne by his family.

Our repast was truly joyous; but some sad and solemn feelings clouded our happiness before we parted: they reverted to the memory of Scharnhorst. Blücher spoke; and I never listened to words so eloquent as he used when he painted in glowing tints the character and services of the hero. The almost involuntary rush of language was the outpouring of poetry itself. At the conclusion he called to him the son of the great departed, who, though used to conceal his feelings under a calm exterior, could scarcely support his emotions as he stood before the aged leader and orator.

After the Battle of Wartenburg we were in Düben. Gneisenau ordered me to proceed through Dessau to Halle; he thought correctly that I might gather some useful information in a district which was so well known to me. Dessau was full of Russians, who crowded the streets and squares. The father of my friend Von Raumer informed me minutely of the enemy's movements; no one could be better able to do it than he. The old notorious Duke of Dessau was no tender master. He had so tyrannized over the proprietors of the land, that he had compelled them one after another to sell to him their properties, so that his dukedom had extended to a considerable territory. The elder Von Raumer was his agent, and conducted all his affairs.

I went to Giedichtenstein, and surprised my father-in-law not a little by my appearance. He was very uneasy, as the enemy had only lately left the village, and were still near, while no troops of ours were in sight. I calmed him by the assurance that I should soon be followed by the Russians.

My sensations may be imagined on entering Halle under such circumstances. Blanc was no longer there, but I learnt that he had escaped from prison, and had joined the army as chaplain. The town, which had been the scene of my brightest and most hopeful days, and in which I had since passed four sad years of danger and wretchedness, I now saw once more, while my actual condition was a strange contrast to that of either period. The town had suffered much, and was in great excitement. It was known how the main army advanced and concentrated itself; how the enemy drew all his forces towards Leipzig, and that a great battle might be expected.

I was but one day alone in Halle before Blücher took up his headquarters there. Gneisenau occupied my old dwelling, and it seemed strange to see him in that former retreat of household joys and cares.

Napoleon moved with a part of his army as if he intended to threaten Berlin, believing that he should be able to disarrange our plans, and compel us to break up our concentrated position. Had he carried out his views, Berlin would have been given up to him. But the strong mind of Germany, which now ruled in our army, was too bold and wise to be deceived. We foresaw that, if our combined forces stood firm, he must abandon his design; he could not spare a portion of his army from the coming struggle, on which his future—his very existence might be staked. A few detachments, therefore, only watched his march, which he soon discontinued. The great day thus approached which was to seal the fate of Germany.

CHAPTER 11

Battle of Leipzig
1813

Early in the morning of the 16th of October I found myself at headquarters near the village of Lindenthal. The day was bright and mild: it is remarkable that every engagement in which I have been present has taken place in the finest weather. Behind us lay a wood, before us an extensive plain. The enemy were posted towards Möckern, on which point we were advancing. The battle began and we were already under a hot fire when Gneisenau despatched me to seek out the Crown Prince of Sweden, who held himself in the rear somewhere near Halle, and entreat him to advance without delay with his Swedes. I had much trouble in finding him, no one knew his exact position, and it was not till night that I made him out at Landsberg in miserable quarters surrounded by Swedish officers. He lay on a mattress spread on the floor of a desolate, nearly empty room; the dark Gascon face, with the prominent nose and the retiring chin, was sharply relieved against the white bedclothes and the laced nightcap.

Gneisenau had explained to me fully the positions of both armies, and how the enemy, consisting of the choicest troops and the Imperial Guard, headed by Napoleon in person, were pressed back by us on Möckern, where the chief contest would take place. The Crown Prince listened attentively whilst I explained all this in my own language and his adjutant translated it to him. He then sat up in bed and made a very long speech, which concluded with a promise to march directly with his troops, and he dismissed me.

Only half of Gneisenau's commission, however, was fulfilled. I had orders to mix among the Swedish soldiers, for he reckoned on my being able to make some impression on them through my native language. An opinion prevailed at headquarters that the Crown Prince had no great liking to take part in a battle which threatened a signal overthrow to his own countrymen, and Gneisenau thought that I might rouse the ardour of the troops. I was to remind them of their great King Gustavus Adolphus, and of his glorious Battle of Leipzig, and to urge that on the same field the fate of Germany was now to be decided, under our generals as it had been then under their great hero.

I held all possible converse during the night with both men and officers, when I found that the order to march had preceded me. Many were already moving off, but some officers remained indolently looking on when all was ready waiting for further orders. Talking with these I perceived that the war had no national interest for the Swedes; they could not see why they should be pressed into a struggle in which they were quite unconcerned, their country not being in danger; the sacrifice was too hard upon the poor Swedes; besides, the small force they could produce would be lost among the mass of nations now armed against Napoleon. I tried to persuade them that the renown of their leader would influence and strengthen the whole allied army.

I cannot praise myself for this part of my argument; I spoke it against my own conviction; my German feelings gave the proud lie to this acknowledgment of superiority in a Frenchman; indeed we always held that the victory at Dennewitz was due alone to General Bülow. Nor had I much to boast of in the way of impression made upon the Swedes; the elements of heroism were not in them, and my declamations on the scene of the approaching battle, and the great deeds there performed by their Gustavus Adolphus, did not help the cause much, for it had of late become rather the fashion in Sweden to disparage the merits of that hero.

Towards noon, however, the Swedish troops were all on the march, and as I learned that this was to be a day of rest I gave my exhausted horse some refreshment. It was dusk when I perceived the Prussian troops on a height near Möckern. I learnt then the issue of the engagement, which had been the fiercest of the whole campaign. It was usual with General v. York to be irresolute before he determined on an attack—once resolved, he ventured everything. The struggle before Möckern had been with Napoleon himself and his finest troops; he had offered battle; the victory was long doubtful; all the first engaged fell; new troops were continually brought up, and the final triumph was won by the reserve corps.

I found a party of the small remnant of Von York's division in a state of great depression. Evening prayers were being read—glorious as had been the victory, the dreadful loss filled every heart with sadness. It was there that, face to face with Napoleon, the Prussians had thirsted to redeem the shame of former times, and had rushed madly on the enemy. The account of the battle of Möckern as given from headquarters was singularly short; it was contained in a few lines, and the heroism displayed, and the important consequences which promised to result from it, were scarcely noticed.

On the second day, between that and the great battle of Leipzig, an attack of cavalry took place under General Wassiltschikof, which was duly praised. It was plainly intended to pass slightly over the Prussian exploits and to bring forward those of the allied Russians as much as possible. I inquired the way to Blücher's headquarters, and rode towards it in the dusk over the fields; after a few steps my horse reared, I could not tell why; my servant alighted and found a corpse in the way. I had to cross the field of battle, and could scarcely get on, the bodies lay so thick; my horse, obliged to face it, left off shying after a time, and I only perceived that I was passing one of the slain by his quietly turning out of the way. I saw bivouac-fires before me, but in the oppression of the scene I had forgotten my direction, and I doubted whether they belonged to our own troops or the enemy's—still I rode towards the fires; living men, whether friends or foes, were welcome.

I reached a wide road and recognised the Russians. Naked men appeared by the bivouac-fires, who looked like giants against the brilliant light: they were engaged in a curious process of purification—they had taken off their shirts to pass them rapidly over the flames. I approached one to inquire where I should find Blücher; he did not understand, but, cheered by the sound of voices, I rode on. I had passed the Russian fires and had been called to by a guard whom I answered without taking much notice, when I heard a voice behind me, and understood the question "Where are you going?" I turned round and learnt that in a few more steps I should have heard the "*qui vive?*"

It was late at night, our horses were quite tired out, myself the same; so I thankfully accepted the invitation of a Russian artillery officer to pass the night in his company. The party were gathered round a gun. Hunger made a slight meal very acceptable, and though we heard skirmishings at the outposts we fell quietly to sleep.

At early dawn we received a morning salutation from the enemy in the form of some cannon-balls, which flew in high arches over our heads. The terrors of the evening, with the wild dreams of the night, vanished before the coming day, and the remembrance of the great stake which that day was to decide met me in all its power. Soldiers stretched at length round the fires were lying all round me, and as I proceeded I found them collecting more and more into groups, preparing for the expected battle.

Blücher's headquarters were in the village of Möckern; all were yet sleeping when I got there. It would convey a false idea of the scene in Blücher's vicinity were it to be supposed that anything like haste or confusion was to be perceived there. Though so great a battle was certain to be fought—though all felt that on its issue the fate of the whole war depended, there was yet no trace of any such important crisis near the great commander. Every officer rose and dressed himself leisurely and carefully; the few washing utensils at command were taken to the wells, and when used by some were instantly claimed by the servants of others to be replenished.

The windows were opened and laid back on the walls, to serve for looking-glasses. Coffee was brought in; some drank from the cups and some from the saucers. Any little difficulty or accident was seized on to give a cheerful turn to the remarks, but these were never extended to the great event which was impending; they spoke on indifferent subjects, even of gay recollections, and a joke was seized on and passed round with thankful eagerness; to a superficial observer they might have seemed like men who were preparing to pursue a journey, and were amusing themselves with the little miseries of an uncomfortable night's lodging.

On that day we did not move out very early. Blücher had joined himself to General Langeron's division, and we found these preparing to pass the Parthe. On the other side of that river the ground rises; there a wonderful spectacle presented itself.

Over the long distant line of rising ground we beheld the French army in movement, and it soon covered the whole range of hills. It was the multitude bound to the man who had subdued the continent and ruled it so long by the terror of his name, now led by him to battle. The columns continued to emerge from the eastern horizon; infantry, cavalry, and artillery glided along in order, and now and then the arms glanced in the newly-risen sunbeams. The whole army seemed like a mighty vision in a dream; fresh hosts continued to rise in the east; still they continued to vanish from our sight far to the west, as the great unbroken mass moved on and on.

We stood long in breathless amazement; then it was that Müffling gave the name to the approaching fight—he called it the great "Nation's battle" (*Völkerschlacht*): the name now belongs to history. We were posted on a plain many miles in extent; troops were round us in every direction. General von York was fighting before Leipzig with the remains of his valiant corps. All around we heard the roar of fierce engagement, but we saw nothing, and remained there stationary the greater part of the day; while adjutants, who were constantly sent to the different corps, brought us back, every few minutes, reports of the progress of the fight from every point.

More than 300,000 men were brought by the allies into the field; 170,000 fought against us. Our ground, as I have said, was a large open plain. Leipzig lay just before us in the distance. It was a strange day to me, passed in such perfect rest in the very centre of a great battle; but the hours flew rapidly; the constant arrival of news kept us in such intense excitement. We heard that at Möckern the enemy had attacked Blücher's division, considering it justly as the centre point of the great moral strength of our whole army.

Napoleon himself led on the attack; he believed that any advantage gained over the most renowned of his enemies would help to subdue the spirits of the whole host. He then brought a half-dispirited army to meet an immensely superior force, yet his great mind had still power to animate his troops; he knew the greatness of the stake. His soldiers fought as daringly as if sure of victory. I must pay the homage of admiration to a hero who made his effort for existence with such daring courage.

This battle also was fought under a brilliant sky. One of the scenes of that eventful day was striking. We discerned a large body of cavalry advance from the enemy's lines in perfect order. There were no troops immediately near the point they advanced upon, and we waited quietly for their coming up; no doubt Blücher was advised of their intentions. They proved to be the Saxon cavalry, who had left the enemy and come over to us. They stood looking resolved, but, as I thought, humbled before us. The commander came forward and approached Blücher, who received him with dignity.

The Saxon officer stated that they had long waited for the moment when they might free themselves from the compulsion of bearing arms against their countrymen; it had come at length. Yet they craved one indulgence: they wished *not* to fight in that battle. Their unhappy king was in Leipzig, in a house in the great market-place, which would soon be in our power. Blücher addressed them shortly, but very kindly, granted their request, and appointed them a position behind the army. I felt for them as they marched by; I imagined all the distress of their position. But all the events of that day, from the first, when the great host passed before my wondering sight, up to that last scene, seemed like a splendid act in a Shakespearian drama, suddenly grown into a living truth.

Till now I had taken no part in the active duties of the day. Blücher, having despatched all the rest of his staff, turned to me at last. "Mr. Professor," he said, "go instantly to General Langeron, take him orders to storm that village; he must expect no help by reinforcement, but the enemy must be dislodged immediately." I hastened off; there was no doubt of the direction I was to take. Langeron had been long disputing Schönfeld; he had been several times in possession of it, and the enemy had retaken it as often, and the flames of the burning village showed me the way. I found him amongst the outermost houses, he was a stern-looking man with a commanding person.

The enemy was again master of the greater part of the place; surrounded by fires the Russians were still fighting obstinately; it was a strange exciting scene, friend and foe in fierce contest, lighted up by the raging flames. I delivered my orders; the general answered despondingly, "My men have fought for many hours, their numbers are thinned, they are tired and exhausted; I cannot withstand the enemy without support." I was compelled to tell him that he must expect no aid, and that the orders to take the place were peremptory; he reflected for one moment, and then gave the word of command for storming.

Every man who was not at that moment actually engaged sprang forward from all sides instantly; the storming party rushed onwards with a loud cry; the enemy could not stand against it, and, the fortune of the day turning everywhere against them, they abandoned the village to the conquerors. I took part with the general in this attack, and when the village was in our power and the enemy in full retreat I hastened back with the news to Blücher. At last I had been engaged—I had been a real sharer in the dangers of the day—but my duty had been so circumscribed, the moment of attack was so exciting, the struggle so short and decisive, that I had not been conscious of the danger till it was past.

When I returned with the report to Blücher, he was already fully aware of the result; he had known it, in fact, sooner than Langeron himself, since from a distance he had been able earlier to distinguish the retreating movement of the enemy.

I was again at our central position, at that point of rest where we had remained throughout the day. Accounts now came in thicker of the general and glorious result of the contest. Evening was coming on, and we left our post and advanced slowly towards Leipzig; suddenly a loud cry, as from thousands of voices, resounded in the air; news came that our troops were pressing into the suburbs, and that the enemy were still defending themselves desperately in the streets and gardens. We galloped forward and were soon up with our fighting troops.

I received orders to join General Wassilschikof, who was appointed, with his cavalry, to pursue the flying enemy. I left the horrible distraction of the general fight and slaughter in the suburbs, and rode, as directed, to Skeuditz. I found that place full of Russian troops which had taken part in the day's conflict, and I was deafened, by certain German-speaking Russian officers, with histories of particular feats and combats. I was told there that a young Dane had fallen fighting valiantly, and learned with surprise and sorrow that his name was Oersted; he was the third and youngest brother of my celebrated countryman.

I could not doubt that it was my friend, though I little expected to hear of him among the Russian army. His death was sad news to me. It was a strange transition in my feelings, strained as they had been to the highest pitch by national events of overwhelming interest, and thus suddenly thrown back into the closer and dearer circle of private sympathy; thoughts sprang quickly up of quiet days gone by, of rest, and home, and friendship, all in painful contrast with the turmoil of the scene around me.

We received news of the flight of the enemy. Wassilschikof moved on early next morning from Skeuditz towards Markranstadt, and passed the night between the 19th and 20th in the neighbourhood of Lützen; between that place and Weissenfels we came up with the last of the retiring army, and were then for the first time aware of the almost inconceivable results of the victory of Leipzig. I there witnessed what quite consoled me for having been obliged to join the Russians,—the extraordinary effectiveness of the *Cossacks* in harassing the rear of a flying army.

The road to Weissenfels lies over a wide plain; we saw the last of the French troops before us; though in hasty flight, they kept tolerably good order; it was rather a misty morning, and there was nothing to be seen between us and the retreating enemy; all at once we perceived *Cossacks* in every direction, singly, or by twos or threes: in an instant they were joined into a troop, in another they were down upon the enemy: these consisted of the tired and weary who were not able to keep up with the rest; the *Cossacks* rushed in between them and the main body, and they were instantaneously surrounded and cut off from it; the rear-guard paused a moment—turned, formed front without advancing, and began a rather brisk fire; but the distance was too great for it to reach us.

The *Cossacks* and their prisoners had disappeared, as if by magic; only here and there we could distinguish a single *Cossack* keeping watch upon the enemy. The retreating guards dared not linger for another fire; they turned their backs on us again and proceeded. This scene was often repeated—the sudden appearance of the *Cossacks*; the cutting off the lingering troops; the guard provoked to defend them, finding by the time they had faced us no object to receive their fire— was acted over and over again; and in the short distance between Lützen and Weissenfels General Wassilschikof took in this way two thousand prisoners, without any real skirmish taking place.

The fugitives hurried forward, and when we reached the suburbs of Weissenfels we found the town occupied by the French: we saw them in the act of passing the Saale by a bridge of boats. Blücher and his staff appeared at this moment; I joined him, and we mounted the heights behind the town, which run parallel with the river. The enemy had just time to withdraw their floating-bridge, and they drew up on the other side of the river opposite to us.

We gave them a heavy cannonade from our heights. The mist cleared off: the bridge of boats which was constructed on our side soon reached across the stream, and the enemy, who then took to flight in great disorder, could not hinder our troops from landing. This was not the only affair during the pursuit: they were constantly attacked, and fled faster and faster; and, as we followed them from Weissenfels to Freiburg, we witnessed fearful traces of the general consternation. I shall never forget the sight: weapons thrown away to lighten their speed—guns, ammunition-waggons, carriages of all descriptions, even some handsome travelling equipages—plainly abandoned because the tired horses could no longer draw them—remained in close confusion, not only on the road, but in the fields, as far as the eye could reach in the direction of the flight. The way was often quite impassable, and we had to make considerable circuits to get on. The enemy themselves had entirely disappeared, at least I saw not one.

When we reached Freiburg we learnt that Napoleon had remained there some hours: it was said that he had been seen at a window, his head resting on his arm in silent despair: Berthier sat opposite to him in a similar state; neither spoke, and officers who entered were silently ordered, by a wave of the hand, to leave the room. The inhabitants were full of anecdotes to prove the desponding state of the flying foe.

We paused but a short time in Freiburg: exhausted by the pursuit, we ascended wearily some considerable heights beyond the town, and in the evening reached the castle of Count Werther Benchlingen. The count was absent, but the countess received Blücher, and made hospitable arrangements for us all. I had retired to the room assigned to me, to make my appearance as fit as my scanty means permitted for a lady's presence, and on my return found Blücher in great indignation. A pamphlet had been found in the castle, written by Professor Crome of Giessen: the title, if I remember right, was *Germany's Rescue through the Battle of Lützen*; and it spoke of the battle as a signal victory for Napoleon, which rendered all further resistance impossible, either from Prussians or Russians.

It is very likely that the bulletins did so misrepresent the affair, but the German professor, however, had dilated on the happy prospects of his country, and stated that all impediments to the full development of the conqueror's wise designs were at last removed. I did not read it through, but it may be conceived how calculated it was to excite the anger of Blücher and his companions. They proceeded to infer the disposition of their hostess from the writing found in her house, and while they were giving vent to their displeasure she presented herself in the midst—a graceful, noble-looking woman, still in the prime of life. Blücher greeted her courteously but coldly, and when she perceived me she approached and spoke to me as an old acquaintance. I recognised in her one of two sisters of a distinguished family of Gotha; they had been much at the court at Weimar, were highly cultivated women, and had been welcomed in Goethe's circle.

I was surprised to see her as our hostess, and perplexed and distressed by the unpleasant suspicions which were entertained against her sentiments. At length she left us, and Blücher ceased to restrain his anger; the remembrance of the absurd scene with the abbess at Radmeritz came over him, and, half in joke and half in scorn, he said, "You seem to be everywhere in favour with the ladies—so this patriotic dame is also a friend of yours."

I tried to convince him that the fact of a book being found in her house did not prove that she participated in the sentiments it contained. Blücher held to his opinion, but when the lady was present he did not forget the courtesy due to a gentlewoman and his hostess. I spoke again to her before we left the castle, and told her of the misunderstanding which the discovery of the book had caused: she laughed, and said there were strange mistakes in times like those; the work had attracted notice by its audacity, but in Gotha and Weimar there was no fear that such sentiments should be entertained.

Under the idea that Napoleon would try to maintain a position, if only for a short time, at Erfurt, Blücher abandoned the immediate pursuit in order to cross over by Langensalza towards Eisenach, and so intercept him. This proved a mistake. Napoleon's loss at Leipzig had been so great, that he could not feel safe till he reached the other side of the Rhine. We made continual marches, tedious from their uniformity: that part of the route between Eisenach and Fulda was remarkable as displaying frightful traces of the defeat which the enemy had suffered.

The rapidity of their flight had completely exhausted the greater part of the army: we saw at first single Frenchmen lying among the bushes; as we proceeded the number of the exhausted, dying sufferers increased, and we found large groups of dead and dying; it was painful to me to observe that they looked upon it as a greater evil to be discovered by us, though we offered them assistance, than to be left to perish with hunger and exhaustion amongst the underwood. I confess I wished myself away from the horrid scene, it was more terrible to me than the violence of the fiercest battle.

Many letters fell into our hands of French correspondence, as well as some from Germans to the French; they sometime furnished us with useful intelligence, but oftener related to private histories. Not a few tales of scandal came thus to light and we read the tender sorrows of German ladies whose French lovers were compelled to depart to meet the dangers of the war I felt ashamed at the way these disgraceful liaisons were paraded for the general amusement. Another booty fell into our hands which entertained us—a great number of Westphalian orders which had been sent to decorate the brave victors in expected fields of glory.

The conquerors had vanished, and the symbol of their triumphs fell to our share; as for the kingdom of Westphalia, we regarded it as a ghost which was already laid. We passed one night at the residence of a prince who was supposed to be in the French interest. Our host had the bad taste to appear before Blücher wearing a Westphalian order so we in return wore our captured medals, not at the button-hole, but at our watchchains.

From Fulda we marched over the waste and wretched district of the Vogelgebirge, where, besides every kind of inconvenience, we had to strive with hunger; it was a happy sight to behold ourselves in the smiling neighbourhood of Giessen, where we refreshed ourselves a day or two.

At Giessen, Blücher found that Professor Crome, the author of the pamphlet before alluded to, had fled on the approach of his troops; he ordered me to inform the senate of the University that the professor might return unmolested. "It is indifferent to us," he said, "what such a scamp may think." I thought that the expression betrayed more annoyance than I could well account for from so great a man, especially when in the full tide of success.

I was requested to deliver an address in Giessen to animate he people in favour of the war. The enemy had many supporters m the southern districts, which bordered on their own territory, and it must be confessed that many oppressive abuses had been remedied under their government, and that their admirers boasted of these reforms. I remember indulging in a paradox in the course of my speech: "If their measures" have been the wisest possible, if the hardships relieved by those pleasures have been in the extreme unbearable, it is now all the more your duty to fight against them to the death, and drive them from the land; for it is treason, it is the lowest depth of degradation, to accept a benefit from an enemy." What persuasion followed my oration I cannot say, as we shortly after quitted the place, but, as regards my own feelings, I do not boast of it; the paradox did not satisfy myself.

The news of General Wrede's great victory over Napoleon at Hanau reached us at Giessen. The southern states of Germany had joined us, and this further success laid the whole country open to us as far as the Rhine. After so many rapidly succeeding engagements, the necessity of reinforcing our strength was apparent, and another armistice was equally required by both armies.

CHAPTER 12

Entering France
1814

I received an agreeable commission from Blücher, confided to me probably at Gneisenau's instigation. Westphalia was nearly without troops; ours had not been stationed there, and the small number of the French remaining in that country were in a critical position. The province had always been favourably disposed towards Prussia, and the enemy was nowhere more thoroughly hated; my duty was to win over and organize the inhabitants. I was instructed to raise the Prussian eagle in all the towns, and to name provisional governments.

My army, with which I was to conquer Westphalia, consisted of two men; my third follower had deserted. My servant composed my staff, and thus equipped I advanced towards a province which was still in possession of the enemy. It was late in the evening when I entered Marburg, and found there were no military in the place. I took up my quarters in an inn, and on arrival soon caused great excitement, as I was the first person who had come from the victorious army. My host, who received me with enthusiasm, informed me that the professors of the university were assembled at a place close by—it was their club evening. I hastened to join them, and was received with acclamations, while the idea that my voice was the first to announce the dawn of liberation filled me with emotion.

I saw Tenneman for the first time: I did not, it is true, share his views on philosophy, but I honoured his powers of deep research, and his quiet joy at my arrival touched my feelings. Wachler also was there and among those already known to me was Niemeyer's son once my pupil at Halle. That our evening was not passed in discussing science may well be guessed. Recollections of the wretched years of bondage which they had suffered, stories of the incapacity of the paltry King, and of the grievances of his misgovernment, were the subjects of their conversation: they added assurances of the strong attachment of the people to their legitimate ruler, and the long-smothered flame of patriotism burst freely out. It was late when I was told that a large number of the inhabitants wished to wait upon me in my own quarters and I left the meeting hastily to receive them.

I heard a great commotion and perceived the sky illuminated by a torchlight procession; the crowd and clamour were immense as they approached the house. I felt instantly how unfitting it would be to receive the demonstration as a compliment to myself: I therefore asked for wine, and rushed among the people, who opened out a circle for me. I called out for silence, and it was wonderful how, first near, and then farther and farther off, the clamour ceased, till all was still from the spot where I stood in the blaze of torches so the distance which was lost in gloom. Then I raised my glass and cried, "To your old ruler, your faith to whom has won you the praise and love of all Germany: long live the Elector!" and I emptied the glass.

The uproar was prodigious: I perceived that it arose from genuine feeling—complaints were mixed with cries of burning hatred against the enemy and of devotion to the rightful prince. I again called for silence, and spoke this time full and freely; it was no constrained oration s at Giessen—I gave full utterance to the sentiments which inspired myself. I withdrew while the acclamations were deafening; deputations waited on me; the future should prove, they said, that my favourable opinion of their sincerity in the great cause was not misplaced. I heard afterwards that numbers, both citizens and students, joined the army: Niemeyer was among the volunteers.

I traversed the Hessian country, passed through Corbach and over the lovely hill-country, and reached Arnsberg. All there were glad to see the first Prussian officer, and shortly after my arrival there was a grand ceremony to welcome me, in which young ladies brought me garlands and presented me with verses; but I had to learn how little one should trust to the bright prospects of the hour. The important part I had to play had begun under these flattering auspices. I trusted that the enthusiasm would spread rapidly through all Westphalia. A proclamation was soon written, printed, and posted in the streets; all was going on charmingly, when news arrived of the approach of General Borstel and his division.

Towards evening on the second day he entered, and I, the volunteer officer charged with important business, dwindled in an instant into my proper character of a very inefficient second-lieutenant.

For another month I was useful in a different way. When I had reported General Borstel's arrival, I received orders to remain, while the truce lasted, in Westphalia, and assist in organising the militia: in the course of that duty I visited Dortmund, In Dortmund I was also requested to address the inhabitant on the subject of the war; how I allowed myself to be persuaded to do it I cannot tell. The public feeling was as well-disposed as possible, the arming of the militia was proceeding rapidly, all the men were rushing to the war, and all the women were enthusiastic in the cause.

I confess that I do not revert to the absurd scene which took place at my address without considerable shame I was first surprised by seeing a crowd of elegantly dressed ladies thronging into the gaily lighted hall; then I had to endure an address, in which I was held up as a subject of envy for being called to inflame the conquering army like another Tyrtaeus. I was not at ease when I spoke, yet I fell better into my subject than I had done at Giessen; my vexation, however, was complete at the conclusion. A number of fair young damsels approached, embraced me in succession, and tried by force to place a crown upon my brow. My philosophy could not resist the salutes, but the crowning was too much; the scene was like a bad frontispiece to some patriotic romance, and the thought of Blücher and his contempt of my Radmeritz honours finished to overwhelm me. It was not till I found myself alone in my room after a good supper, that I was sufficiently recovered to laugh heartily at the ludicrous performance.

The organization of the militia was soon so complete that I was able to proceed to Dusseldorf, where, by Blücher's orders, I was to act in concert with my friend Justus Grüner. Grüner had been seized by the Austrian government while residing in Bohemia, and had been imprisoned in a fortress in Hungary; his name and position had been carefully concealed, and, being very fair, many had supposed him to be the exiled King of Sweden. He was liberated when Austria joined us, and when our armies had cleared the country as far as the Rhine he was sent to Dusseldorf as Governor of the district; he occupied the palace which had been used by the French governor Beugnot, who held the appointment under Joachim, King of Naples: it was a splendid mansion, fitted up with Parisian elegance; a spacious and richly furnished suite of rooms was assigned to my use, and servants appointed to attend me. Grüner liked a good table, and had an excuse for indulging in his fancy, since persons of distinction were continually arriving, whom it was necessary to entertain. Thus I found a new and surprising phase of the ever-varying fortunes of war. I passed two delightful months in Dusseldorf.

Among the distinguished persons whom I met at Grüner's table was the present Duke of Coburg. I remember a conversation which I held with him one day after dinner, on the wish which then generally prevailed for a closer reunion of the German empire. I was surprised to hear him argue that it was desirable to suppress or merge the smaller States, through which the strength of the empire was broken up. Whether he thought his own dominions safe, or whether by his disinterested speech he meant to discover my private opinions, I cannot tell; I was quite decided against remodelling the empire according to the crotchet which filled people's heads at the time, which was to give a German constitutional monarchy, with a great metropolis like Paris or London; and I stated my objections.

"My wish," said I, "to see Germany composed of so many separate States is not altogether disinterested, it affects men of science too nearly. The progress of free and individual intellectual development spends on such an arrangement now in Germany as it did in former times in Greece; the contracted views which pervade all English and French literature are owing to the influence exercised in the capitals of those countries. At this moment I can instance a philosopher, who, restricted in the free dissemination of his peculiar views in one State, found ready protection in another. Fichte, banished from Jena, found a refuge and freedom in Prussia."

The Duke laughed, and reminded me that he had taken part in suppressing Fichte's teaching. I answered that I was fully aware of the fact, neither was I presuming to censure the decree, but I could not resist so apt an illustration of my argument. On many other occasions I heard opinions from persons of high stations, which I always ventured to resist to the uttermost, since they involved principles which I thought opposed to the complete regeneration of Germany.

In the midst of active business, relating to the re-establishment of the University at Düsseldorf, I was, however, often reminded of the war and of my military duties. One event cast a shadow over that agreeable period; my late connection and regard for Bolkenstern will be remembered; he had won distinction in the late campaign, and commanded two battalions opposite Cologne. While I remained in Düsseldorf he came to that place to visit me, and great was my enjoyment of his society.

A few days after he left me I received news of his death; he had heard of the passage of the army over the Rhine, and, fancying that the enemy were on the point of retiring everywhere, had crossed and attacked them, but with too small a force. General Sebastiani still kept possession of Cologne; Bolkenstern fought with some success on the bank close under the town, but the enemy brought so great a force to oppose him, that he saw no chance of rescuing his men but by a rapid retreat across the river; he was the last to leave the shore, and, all the boats having been filled, he dashed with his horse into the flood meaning to swim over. A shot reached him, and the Rhine was his grave. A monument was erected to him on the Drachenfels.

At length I received orders to rejoin the army, and I left Düsseldorf with regret and passed through Coblentz, rode through the valley of the Moselle to Treves, and there found an order to wait for troops advancing towards the main body, in being forbidden to travel through the enemy's country alone or in only small parties. I found General Dörnberg in a house on the road beyond Grevenmachern; his Hessian troops were investing the fortress of Luxemburg. General Count Haake appeared there shortly after my arrival with some regiments of cavalry which he was conducting to join Blücher, and I entered France in their company.

Our sensations were new and strange as we proceeded into the enemy's country; we felt for the first time thrown back wholly on our own resources, for every inhabitant was a foe determined to injure us how and when he could. I before remarked that the features of a fair landscape are not to be recognised in the time of battle; I now perceived that the face of a hostile land wears a mask to the invader—every house and thicket conceals a danger—every object has an ominous meaning, and this character it never loses.

The first fortress of importance which we had to pass was Thionville. Being in possession of the French, and strongly garrisoned, we had reason to expect that we should be attacked in passing by a superior force, and the nature of the country must render our defence extremely difficult. We arrived late in the evening at Maison Rouge, a place not far from Thionville, and, though we were greatly fatigued, we spent nearly all the night in reconnoitring and making arrangements for marching past the fortress.

I rode out silently with the general and some of his staff; we did not venture to approach near the fortress, and we perceived no troops, but all the intelligence we arrived at increased our fear that the enemy might issue by some defile of which we were ignorant, and come suddenly upon us.

At noon the following day we proceeded between vine-covered hills which rose abruptly on each side; the walls which divided the vineyards and the trees made the sides of the hills impassable for the horses, so that they could proceed only in lengthened file along the narrow pass. Great complaints were uttered, and with reason, that so considerable a body of cavalry should have been sent into a foreign country unaccompanied by infantry, which alone could have acted in such a situation; in fact, had the enemy appeared on the heights above us, we must have fallen helplessly into their power.

The scouts we had sent out brought news that troops were issuing from the fortress; the defile seemed endless, and our sensations were most unpleasant as we rode on slowly and with great difficulty, expecting every instant an attack from above, which we had no means whatever to withstand. At last, after some hours, the road began to ascend, but still we could only ride three abreast between the hills, and a weary anxious time passed before the long procession reached the plain above. I rode about the middle and learnt that the rear-guard was actually attacked, but as we rose upon freer ground we soon galloped out of sight of the enemy, who were on foot; it was under such critical circumstances that we entered the hostile country.

On our further march towards Chalons-sur-Marne we met with no opposition, and as we rode quietly forward we enjoyed a most animated conversation. General Haake was most courteous to me, as well as his officers, among whom I found some highly cultivated men, especially Major v. Kürssel, chief of a battalion; he was fond of poetry, and early in the campaign had composed and arranged some songs to animate his troops; they were soon learnt by every man, and when sung in full chorus, the whole force joining, and the poet himself leading with his fine voice, the effect was truly inspiring.

We had quartered for the night in the small town of Commercy, and by an early march arrived at a place where the road winds spirally upwards round a steep portion of the Sandstone Mountains: before us the cavalry were seen mounting the winding paths of the steep acclivity; their brilliant *cuirassier* uniforms and perfect equipment gave to the scene the character of some splendid pageant. The procession mounted leisurely and in unbroken order, covering the whole face of the ascent; the morning sun shone on their helmets and flashed from their weapons, and as they approached the summit they poured forth a glorious and loud song of triumph, which resounded in rich harmony through the deep vales below, and was returned by many an echo from the distant hills—it was a splendid spectacle.

In Vitry we halted a day, and received the first news of the serious battle fought by General v. York at Château-Thierry; we obtained only broken scraps of news regarding it, which made us anxious about our own position. It was said that a Russian corps had been cut off and nearly dispersed, and this report probably related to that of General Alsusief. Even Blücher's position appeared to us highly critical, and our own advance dangerous, since the whole country was said to be in activity; we knew, however, that it was natural for the inhabitants to try to increase our perplexity by exaggerated statements, and we therefore listened as little as possible to their reports: they actually defied us in Vitry, and it needed all our force to keep their bitter animosity in check.

I was with some officers in a farmhouse near the town, standing in the sitting-room of the owner; the farmer and his wife were both present, talking civilly with us, when an audacious-looking man, apparently a farming-servant, entered; he scarcely noticed us, and in the presence of his master and mistress threw himself with his hat on upon a sofa. This seemed to surprise our host and his wife so little, that, though rather startling to our German ideas, we concluded it must be the custom of the country, and probably one of the consequences of the Revolution, through which many courtesies had been banished from domestic life. The sullen boor at last addressed the host as if we had not been present; he heaped report upon report of our utter defeat in every quarter, and said that Blücher's entire army was destroyed, or flying in wild confusion.

I confess I felt awed by the man's audacity; we pretended, however, not to have heard him, since the remarks were not addressed to us; we pursued our conversation with our host, asked for breakfast, partook of it leisurely, and remained much longer than we had at first intended. That we proceeded towards Châlons with some anxiety may be well imagined, and our anxiety increased on meeting some scattered Russians, who seemed surprised at our composure and the direction in which we marched, it being towards the point from whence they were hastening. They were foot-soldiers, and made us understand that they had received orders to rejoin at a meeting-place farther south, they therefore could not join with us, though they were much exhausted:

we did not dare to alter our course.

It was dark when we reached Châlons, and we did not venture to enter the town, but rested a few hours, meaning to push forward again during the night to Bergières, near Bertus, where Blücher's headquarters were posted. We rode on through the night in continual danger of being attacked; I was in the midst, or, perhaps, farther back, and our march was interrupted almost every minute, but whether by the enemy or by other impediments I could not ascertain. It is esteemed a grave fault, and one which among the men is always severely punished, for a rider to sleep on a march, for the sway of the sleeper's body hurts the horse. I was so thoroughly worn out that it was impossible to keep awake; I therefore got off, as we were going slowly, and many other officers did the same, and we slept as we walked; we were only roused when any impediment caused a halt. The march continued the whole night, and by break of day we were in Bergières, at Blücher's headuarters.

We found all in movement; an advance towards Etoges was projected, but I was completely exhausted, and, throwing myself on the straw which an officer had just left, fell fast asleep, and my servant did the same. A friend had undertaken to waken me in two hours, and though it cost me much to rise and move again, I was strengthened by the sleep, and at length, in company with the advancing staff, was able to greet the friends from whom I had been for three months parted; but our circumstances were so pressing, and demanded so much of our thoughts, that I learned little of the past or of the present position of the enemy, or of the truth of the numerous reports which had reached us.

The usual confidence, however, still reigned in Blücher's party, and I found myself beginning to believe that all was prosperous and hopeful, and even that we were on the certain route for Paris, though we might yet have to fight our way. I heard only vague mention of the battle near Brienne, where it seemed that Blücher himself had been in considerable danger, and had extricated himself with difficulty from the castle where he was attacked. It seemed that he had also escaped a similar danger in Etoges.

I inquired into the changes which had taken place at headquarters since I had been absent. Raumer was there; and to my surprise and joy I found my friend Blaue, he with whom I had shared in all the dangers, fears, and hopes of the unhappy time when Halle was first taken possession of by the enemy and the University dissolved. Since he had been liberated from, prison in Cassel he had sought to obtain an appointment as military chaplain, and by Gneisenau's advice had joined Blücher, ready for any that might become vacant. He wore a dark overcoat, under which a sword was hidden. Thus, in this strange war, we two, a preacher and a philosopher, rode side by side armed for the fight; we were soon absorbed in earnest discussion of the great changes which we and the people had lived to see since we had parted.

It was past noon when we reached Etoges; it appeared to me that fighting was going on in every direction, but we still pressed forward, and quartered for the night in the village of Champaubert, on the broad, but far from well-kept, road on the lesser route to Paris. During the whole war I was never so wholly in the dark as to our place and prospects: our army was scattered about in various parts of northern France; I was destitute of all local knowledge; from the rapidity of our movements I could not refer to maps, and I felt this uncertainty so oppressive that I got little repose though we halted for the night. The troops were again in movement at the earliest dawn; the broad road led through the village, and some detached houses seemed to indicate the approach to Paris: they were not handsome, but had a metropolitan look. I noticed a sign over a house, which in the German language proclaimed it to be a "refuge for wandering tailors:" we were going towards Montmirail.

Blücher had not yet discovered that the Generals v. York and v. Sacken had been forced back beyond the Marne; he believed that he should have been able to co-operate with their divisions, and therefore ventured to defy Napoleon himself, who had concentrated his army near Montmirail. Early in the forenoon we found ourselves on the side of a hill which hid the town from our view. I gathered from some whispers which reached my ears, and from the hasty movements of the adjutants, that Blücher had just learnt that Napoleon held the Marne invested by so strong a force that it was impossible for the Generals v. York and v. Sacken to attempt a passage. A few cannon-shots reached us, and a horseman close to me was struck; I looked involuntarily round, and saw him fall with his head frightfully shattered.

Our retreat began immediately towards Champaubert in perfect order. The hollowed ground did not permit us to see anything beyond us; I could perceive little even of our own troops or of the direction we were taking; but the heavy, constant cannonade, and the riding to and fro of single horsemen of the enemy, convinced me that engagements were taking place all around during the retreat. I was with Blücher and his staff, who, separated from the main body, and escorted by only a few troops, brought up the rear.

Then we saw the enemy on the hills on both sides. Grenades burst close to us; cannon-balls fell thicker into the midst of us; the musketry began, from the closer approach of the enemy, to be destructive; and even some single cavalry soldiers tried to hew their way into the midst of us. They were wrapped in white cloaks, and wore immense bear-skin caps, which half covered their faces. As soon as I was able to observe the small number of troops which accompanied us, and how we were attacked in every way, the extremity of our danger stood revealed to me. Exhausted by the exertions of the previous days, I rode up to Blaue: my field-flask was empty, for I had shared it with many. "Will you bestow one glass on me from yours?" I said to him.

"I will divide all that remains with you," he answered; "it is the last that we shall ever drink together;" and he said this with the greatest calmness possible.

We rode through Champaubert; but before we reached the place many of those bear-skin caps rode close up, as if ready to seize upon us. In that critical moment the personal courage of the great commander blazed forth. "I will give it the fellows," he exclaimed; and we saw him dart upon an approaching horseman. Many hastened after him, but the horseman had fled.

On the other side of Champaubert we were on a meadow which was separated by green hedges from the road on our right. The forest through which the road lay between us and Etoges was at some considerable distance before us; the last retreating Russian guns were just disappearing in the wood; two battalions of Prussian troops were posted to protect us on the meadow, and one cannon served by Russians remained also near us. The enemy pressed on us more and more, and the time seemed near when it would no longer be possible to reach the wood, and get up with the main body. The battalion formed a square, and maintained their position with amazing firmness.

The Russian artillery officer loaded, fired, and loaded again, and was asking Müffling, who was near, which way he had better point the gun, when the cry was suddenly heard, "We must separate; every one must save himself as he can." The first care was by all means to save the leader: the principals must gather round him; the rest make off as they could. Then I heard Müffling shout, "We must all hold together." The staff placed themselves instantly in the ranks; the battalion closed up, determined to risk everything. The Russian officer charged his gun again, and we bore down in full gallop against the enemy, who stood before us. They gave way. I think they had not looked for such a charge. Perhaps in the dusk, which did not admit of ascertaining the extent of our force, they might have supposed that we had received a sudden reinforcement. We reached the wood in safety.

The last Russian guns were passing along the road which led through the forest. We separated again, and made our way singly among the trees as well as we could to the right. On the left the enemy's cavalry tried to press upon us, but the space was too contracted for any general attack, and it was hard to distinguish friends from foes. The Russian artillerymen knocked down many French horsemen with the sponges with which they cleaned their guns.

Our progress thus through the forest in the dark night continued to be highly dangerous; though the thicket partly protected us, we knew not how we might be assailed either in front or rear. I was riding by Colonel Oppen, conversing with him, when some confusion took place behind us. He rode back to inquire the cause, and was never heard of again. Every possible attempt was made afterwards to ascertain when and where he fell, and to discover the body, but in vain. The army lost a most valuable officer, and I a friend.

The forest extends some miles without a break; it took a long time to retreat through it; at first we went slowly, but, though I cannot tell how it was managed, we got forward more and more quickly, and at last rode at full gallop. This fact was denied afterwards, and it was asserted that we never exceeded the usual trot, but I cannot be deceived. I remember my horse participated in the general eagerness to push forward, and being but a bad rider I could not hold him, and I thus became entangled with Count v. G——— , who was very angry, but I had no power to avoid it.

At Etoges the forest ended: we pressed still farther on, reached Bergières, and took possession of the same outworks which we had left two days before; no one troubled himself about anyone else, but sought a resting-place as he could. Since I had left Vitry I had never slept except an hour or two snatched here and there, and I sank upon the hard-trodden ground in utter exhaustion. It was a sleep like death, such as in my whole life I never knew before or after. I felt at first a sensation as of some dreadful oppression, which I strove to resist, but in vain, yet it did not wake me, and I sank deeper and deeper into perfectly unconscious sleep.

It was bright day when I awoke, and looking on the cloak in which I had wrapped myself I perceived stains of blood. I learnt that a man fatally wounded had been laid on some straw close by my side; while his wounds were being dressed he had rolled himself in his death agony upon me—his corpse lay still beside me. This incident, horrible as it was, affected me, after all that I had witnessed, but little, and the sleep had strengthened me astonishingly. I joined the party which surrounded Blücher, and found that the events of the preceding day had been less disastrous than my fears had painted them. The order of our retreat had not been broken, nor was the loss on our side very great.

Amongst those who accompanied our headquarters was Sir Hudson Lowe, who has since been so much blamed for his severity in guarding Napoleon in the island of St. Helena. When I first saw him I was unfavourably impressed by his gloomy countenance, and by the morose silence which he always preserved. On this occasion he was entirely changed. The dangerous day, the discipline kept unbroken by the troops in the most threatening circumstances, the courage, the endurance displayed by all, seemed so admirable to the brave Englishman, that he dwelt on the recollection of it. His voice was now free and loud in praise.

A most animated account was sent by him to the English newspapers of what we call the battle of Champaubert; in the French bulletins it is named the Battle of Montmirail. He appeared truly amiable on that occasion, and I have since always been ready to join those who have of late spoken freely in his defence. I believe, with them, that though cold in manner and inexorable where duty required him to be severe, he was really kinder and gentler than he appeared.

We retired still farther towards Châlons at our leisure; the pursuit was not continued; the divisions of Generals v. Sacken and v. York joined, and were united under the immediate command of Blücher. General v. York had retired earlier on Châlons, but had already left the place again when we entered it. We remained there some days in perfect quiet; I found myself again amongst my friends, C. v. Raumer, Blaue, and Stetzer, one of my former intimates in Halle. Many were the topics of absorbing interest which we discussed, and the sparkling champagne helped to raise our spirits. The hours flew like minutes.

The Prussians at first only looked upon the champagne as a sort of light beer. It happened that General v. York was blockading the town while Macdonald occupied it. V. York had separated from the latter general in the Russian campaign, and thereby had caused the outbreak of the definitive war. The blockading troops discovered a number of wine-cellars near the walls, which they broke into, and the quantity consumed was prodigious, the men having no idea of the power of the wine.

When my friend Willison, who was adjutant to the general, went to inspect the outposts, he found the whole army in sleepy intoxication. General v. York laughed when it was reported to him, but his situation in the face of an enemy who would gladly have snatched a much-longed-for revenge, was serious enough. The quantity of champagne which was consumed that winter was wonderful; on the bare and dreary plains round Châlons we found the remains of broken bottles in such thick quantities as to be dangerous to the horses.

CHAPTER 13

Napoleon's Chance Neglected
1814

The marches and counter-marches of our winter campaign in France were so alike, that, even were I able to record them all from memory, the recital would but prove uninteresting. A few sketches of the leading features will suffice.

We learnt by degrees how falsely our state after the Battles of Brienne and Montmirail had been represented at Napoleon's headuarters. At first we heard it only by reports, but, when some numbers of the *Journal de l'Empire* fell into our hands,; the reading of the bulletins afforded us immense amusement. By their accounts Blücher's army had been utterly annihilated. The troops under General v. Sacken and General v. York had also, after the battles of Château-Thierry and Montmirail, fled in consternation and been completely dispersed. A countryman and early friend of mine, Malte Brun, was with Napoleon, and as editor of the *Journal de l'Empire* assisted in composing these bulletins. So strangely were men brought into opposition in this singular war.

The service during the inclement season became daily more oppressive to the troops; though no great actions were fought, continual skirmishes were taking place. The cold and wet continued to increase, and sickness prevailed, though I believe even; to a greater degree in the enemy's army than our own. Through the exertions of the commissaries the want of provisions was not much felt generally, but it was severely so at headquarters, arising from the necessity of providing for the men first. It was taken for granted that we could help ourselves, and thus we were often left in urgent want.

Money was sometimes scarce, and often useless when we had it; the villages in which we rested or passed the nights were nearly always deserted by the inhabitants, and sometimes burnt, so that nothing remained but the four walls of a house, and the chimney in the midst. If not destroyed by fire, we thought it a lucky chance when everything was not cleared away. A sack of potatoes, which we could roast in haste by a bivouac fire, was considered a great treasure. I and my friends for long together had nothing else than some slices of bacon toasted at the fire on the end of a stick.

I remember one occasion when we found not only potatoes and an abundance of bacon, but a frying-pan; we feasted delicately and thankfully that day, yet sparingly, having prudent care for the future hour of need. Often as we thus formed a circle round the fire, toasting our bacon, V. Raumer and I used to recur to times of home and comfort, and think how shocked our wives would be were they to see how we then fared: at home such diet would have made me very ill; now, however, all agreed with me, and our spirits seldom failed, particularly when we were on the move. I still wore the uniform which I had brought with me from Breslau. I suffered much from want of change of linen, and the care of my beard was a cruel inconvenience, the accomplishment of shaving being one which I never could acquire.

Nearly all the barbers in the towns were invalided soldiers; they flourished off the beard with a single stroke on each side, and I felt it a very serious affair to trust my throat so to the mercy of a hating enemy. When I did submit, I took care to have a friend present, but I often postponed the ordeal for a week or even a fortnight. Then from my childhood I had been accustomed to the peculiar cleanliness of the northern nations; I was quite unversed in the little practices for making a tidy show—how to bring outwards and make the most of the one little white part of the collar or shirt-front was a mystery to me, for I had learnt the carelessness which results from being really neat I suffered much from these discomforts.

In March, when Napoleon was in our rear and all communication was nearly cut off, our want became greater, and was felt severely amongst the men; the discipline began at the same time to fail; there was plunder everywhere; houses were sacked, and the inhabitants fled; plundering and scenes of violence were not always exercised only on the enemy. I remember once resting for the night at a village which had been deserted; but in a yard of the farmhouse which we entered we found a turkey. Our party, servants and all, consisted of about I fourteen or fifteen.

As we sat round the hearth in the large kitchen, by a bright fire, the pot with water and salt all ready for the turkey to boil all night, that we might enjoy a rich breakfast in the morning, a large party of Russians burst violently in: we tried to persuade them to desist from molesting us, but, though they saw that we were Prussian officers, they attacked us fiercely. We were discreet enough not to meet them with our drawn swords, and I had long observed that my arm was too weak to make any impression on a Russian shoulder; I struck those who came upon me, therefore, crossways on the face. We succeeded in driving them away; but we were assailed on several other occasions, and if the war had lasted much longer it was too plainly to be seen how such outrages would have increased.

More grievances at length oppressed me: there are always at headquarters a number of young men, as geographical engineers, messengers, &c.; these had found employment easily while the war continued in Germany, and was carried on with more care and rule: my position was similar to theirs, and I have to thank the leaders, who were personally acquainted with me and my former position, for having made me useful. In France, however, neither the people just alluded to, nor my friends nor I, could find any useful occupation. This feeling of being useless was truly painful; generals and officers of distinction and their well-informed adjutants formed an exclusive circle; it was right and necessary that they should do so—the time was critical; all resolves had to be carried out on the instant; that which was in contemplation was imparted only to those who ought to know it; it was not mistrust nor changed sentiments which excluded me from the confidence I formerly enjoyed, it was the pressure of the moment.

Yet I felt the position most oppressive: personal inconveniences increased; to make my situation still more embarrassing, the conversation of the young men with whom I was forced to associate wearied me, and, alas! it never ceased. In our marches and counter-marches I was never left alone; six or seven, or even ten or twelve, officers were crowded together in one room, to lie all night on straw; pure air was what I never could dispense with: I remember when in Gotha being nearly killed with suffocation, when I and many others had to enter a wretched room which had been only just left by *Cossacks*, and I was compelled to pass the night leaning out of the open window; in France I was often obliged to do the same.

My companions never ceased their talking till one after another dropped asleep, and changed the chatter into a chorus of continuous snoring; then I usually rose, laid my straw on the floor close to the open door, wrapped myself as well as I could within my cloak, and slept in the intense cold. As this state of things continued, as want of nourishment was added to our other miseries, and as I found that on no occasion could I withdraw to find in solitude means to recruit my shattered powers of thought, I fell into a state which may be described as really out of my senses.

In some handsome *châteaux* everything was destroyed, and many valuables hidden which were soon discovered; in the wine-cellars the doors were generally walled up, but it was easy to detect the new mortar, and indeed it proved more a temptation than a safeguard; these places were generally all discovered and plundered before the headquarters arrived. Some of the *châteaux*, with the ruined remains of elegance and luxury, were a sad spectacle. We took possession of one where the care to render everything useless was very striking, even the featherbeds had been cut open, and the rooms were filled with down and feathers: we entered another just as General Brüne's Russians were breaking into the wine-cellars; instead of tapping the large wine-butts, they staved them in, and the soldiers actually waded through a sea of wine to drink it as it flowed from the casks. It has been related that during the Revolution a wine-cellar in Strasburg was attacked, and that a number of people were drowned in the flood of liquor; I believed in the possibility of the story as I looked upon the scene just described.

A very elegant villa, in which we passed the night before our entrance into Meaux, left a vivid impression on my memory, the traces of tasteful luxury and domestic comfort were so striking in the midst of desolation. I fancied that the house had been prepared for an unusual assemblage of guests; in a distant part, removed from the receiving apartments, I found a library, great part of which had been industriously destroyed; the floor was covered with shreds of leaves and torn engravings many empty shelves indicated that a considerable portion of the books had been conveyed away; yet everything gave evidence of a sudden flight which had stopped the process of removal.

Concealed by a tapestry-covered door, I at length discovered the entrance to an enchanting *boudoir*, it remained untouched, exactly as the occupant had left it. It was circular, and surrounded by soft couches; opposite to each other were two copies of antique statues—the Apollo and the Gladiator; an elegant *fauteuil* stood near the window, and on the table near it lay open the *Memoirs of Cardinal Retz*; writing materials were ready for use, and some pencils lay beside a half-copied drawing.

Amongst the rich trifles which covered the table was a note, apparently written in haste, on the subject of the approaching danger. I was still more surprised, as I passed into another chamber, to find statues, casts of limbs, modelling clay, and all the arrangements of a sculptor's studio. For many hours I was lost in contemplating this sanctuary of refinement—the abode of peace and cultivation; and I confess that I was attracted towards the possessor with feelings of sympathy and admiration, which were at strange variance with the national hatred which we had brought with us into France.

In general, however, the dwellings in the smaller towns were very unlike that which I have described; the greater number had been emptied, like the village cottages, and the bare cold chambers afforded scarcely more comfort than the bivouac. The cold during that winter was sometimes intense, and fuel often failed. I remember, late one evening, entering one of those rooms in Mery, when I was nearly frozen; we searched the house through for fuel, and found none; at last we determined to burn the few remaining chairs and tables: the destructive work must be done by ourselves, for the servants were engaged with the horses.

I was just on the point of breaking up a chair, when it struck me that my character of a middle-aged philosopher was in too glaring contrast with my occupation. I remembered the ominous words of Gneisenau, when, before the battle of Bautzen, he alluded to the state into which we all might lapse, should the war be long protracted. I thought of the daily falling off in discipline, and that the means of preserving what remained was continually growing weaker; I refrained from assisting the growing evil by my bad example, and the chair was saved.

It was a subject of surprise to me that Napoleon did not continue the pursuit when we retired on Champaubert; had he done so, systematically and with vigour, our danger would have been extreme; he might have prevented our junction with the divisions of Generals v. York and v. Sacken, and thus have almost annihilated Blücher's force. The whole moral spirit which impelled the war would have sunk with him, our previous successes all have been reversed, and we might have been obliged, first, to accept a truce, and then an ignominious peace. This idea depressed me greatly, and it was therefore an unspeakable relief to my mind when the pursuit ceased; not only because we were relieved from the imminent personal peril, but because it betrayed great want of power and resolution in the enemy.

I have since heard many well-judging officers assert that Napoleon's want of resolution to follow up a line of conduct which must have com- passed our destruction could only be explained by his having lost, after the battle of Moscow, all his former faith in his own invincibility; the hasty flight after the Battle of Leipzig would never have taken place had his old spirit not deserted him.

A considerable engagement took place before the town of Mery-sur-Saône; we abandoned the town, through which the high road to Paris forms a wide street, because the resistance before it was too strong. The place was burning, and the ammunition-waggons were drawn through the flames. In the evening we reached St. Anglure; the houses which surrounded the castle were also burning, and the showers of sparks were sent in glowing arches in every direction; for the second time that day our ammunition-waggons were exposed to the danger of explosion. I thought little of it then, but the remembrance afterwards gave rise to some curious reflections.

I have often noticed how seldom a cannon-ball hits in the midst of a close conflict, while in peaceful times the chance shot from a fowling-piece finds its certain victim; so the myriads of sparks, free to light in every direction, seemed to withdraw and spare the powder. I do not remember, in the whole war, to have heard of more than one explosion. We had just entered Meaux, after our whole forces had united to march against Paris; a storm raged without, and there was a perpetual sound of the tramp of horses and the clang of arms; suddenly we heard, above all, a distant, low, tremendous roar, which shook the poor cottage in which we had taken refuge. I never learned whether the disaster occurred amongst us or the enemy.

In St. Anglure some important negotiations were carried on between Blücher and the royal headquarters. Great apprehensions were entertained that we should have to join the main body, in consequence of the losses we had suffered at Brienne, Epernay, Château-Thierry, and Champaubert, and of the exhausted state to which so many marches and unfavourable circumstances had contributed. The main body was near to us in Troyes, and held an extended position southwards. Blücher and his followers were by no means disposed to relinquish the independent position they had maintained.

The proposal was made for Blücher's army to combine with the Netherland forces under Winzingerode and Bülow, and for Blücher to be commander-in-chief over the whole. This was laid before the

Emperor Alexander and the King of Prussia, who were both with the main body. Many were opposed to its reception, and preferred an armistice. Major v. Grolmann, one of the most distinguished officers in the Prussian army, was fully convinced of the necessity of pushing on the war till Napoleon's power should be crushed forever. It had often been stated that the hostility was directed against Napoleon, not against France; and though Blücher did not exactly share that sentiment, he saw that France would be powerless if Napoleon were dethroned.

Though acting in a subordinate capacity, v. Grolmann did much towards the success of the proposal. We had little rest that night in St. Anglure. V. Grolmann was continually flying to and from the royal headquarters. I fancy the plan was then accepted; but until all was finally arranged we continued in suspense. Blücher moved towards La Ferté-sous-Jouarre, where we remained some days.

We were at length ordered to cross the river, and found Blücher in the highest spirits: the order had arrived for him to unite with Bülow and Winzingerode, who were coming from Belgium, and to take independent command of the combined force. The army moved forward; an advance along the Ourcq was attempted, but was given up: it is well known how much this junction was facilitated by the abandonment of Soissons. I can record few incidents of that time; the tremendous crowd as we entered Soissons is the chief point which rests in my remembrance.

When we first joined Bülow's forces the appearance both of officers and men amazed us; they had passed a most comfortable winter in Belgium and the Netherlands, and had been well fed and clothed. What a contrast were Blücher's troops, exhausted by fatigue, marches, and bivouacs, thinned by want of food, and all in rags, and the old shoes worn till they scarcely covered the feet! The contrast with our new comrades made our state seem more pitiable than before.

Every possible exertion was made to reach Laon before Napoleon, who was also eager to advance and obtain possession of it before us: had he been able to do so, our affairs must without doubt have taken a most unhappy turn. On our march towards it, whilst the advanced body of the army was severely engaged before us at Craonne, Blücher's division, in their eagerness to push on, fell into a defile, the danger of which seemed to me terrific. I often thought that our troops were in a most critical position, but they never appeared so much so as at that moment. It struck me as a remarkable fact that, in spite of all efforts to gain intelligence, both parties in a campaign remain strangely ignorant of the real state of the enemy, and that their information generally fails exactly when it is of most importance.

We took possession of Laon. The town stands on a chalk hill which rises abruptly from an extensive plain, which it commands towards the north and west. It is difficult of access on all sides, and, as it was a most important position. Napoleon tried with all his might to force us from it; but the victory we gained there opened the road for us to Paris.

The mode in which I witnessed the Battle of Laon was singular, and at least convenient. We were quartered on a family in the town, and rode out every morning, after a comfortable night's rest and a good breakfast, to the outside of the town, and planted ourselves on the edge of the chalk cliff, from whence we had a perfect view of the whole plain. Not far from the western gate of the town a hollow narrow road leads from the town to the plain beneath; the face of the cliff stretches out towards the left, where the ground is on a level with the town.

General Bülow's division was posted immediately under our heights; Napoleon made repeated attacks on him, and we could observe leisurely the conflicts which took place just under our feet. On the first day our heights were much exposed to the enemy's fire; but the nearness of our artillery and the great altitude of our position made it difficult for the enemy to direct their guns against us.

On the day of the severest fighting, Gneisenau and Müffling sat on chairs placed on the very edge of the precipice; Blücher, if I remember right, was ill, and remained in the town. It was a clear bright spring day; the extensive fruitful plain lay as far as the eye could reach before us strewed with villages. It was not one continued battle, but different corps of the enemy as they came in sight were attacked, and engagements were taking place at several points distinct from each other at the same time. We saw all with perfect ease. Sometimes two masses of infantry were fighting vigorously: we watched in the beginning the doubtful struggle; then we perceived that the victory leaned to our side, and at last that the enemy turned and fled.

Sometimes our cavalry attacked a square, broke through it, and dispersed it. In some of the villages the enemy tried to make an obstinate resistance; we beheld them driven out and fly, while our troops dashed after them. In one place a Russian square was furiously attacked; they were shot at with musket-ball, while a mass of cavalry tried to hew a road into the midst of them; but they were not to be broken; they waved every way, and curved and bent, but always drew closer again into a dense mass as if they had been one single living body. It was a grand, a wonderful sight! They were held together by the strength of perfect obedience; the will of each individual seemed merged into that of the whole mass. The generals themselves viewed the spectacle with amazement; Gneisenau was loud in his delight.

Close behind our seats was a mill; a grenade fell upon the mill and set it on fire; it burned behind our backs: henceforth the cannonade ceased, the enemy had forced their way to the cliff, and almost approached the hollow road; there, just at our feet, a tremendous attack took place from our side; we were obliged to bend over the brink of the precipice to watch the issue of the struggle. The French were driven back.

We were for three days together in this convenient manner spectators of the contest, and when the day's work was over we withdrew to a quiet supper. At the end of the third day Napoleon abandoned the attack and withdrew from before Laon.

A curious escape took place on that occasion, which was told me on such authority that, incredible as it seems, I cannot doubt it. In the heat of an engagement the horse of one of General V. York's officers was struck by a shell; it entered near the shoulder and was buried in the body; the animal made a convulsive spring upwards and threw the rider, the fragments of the shell were projected on all sides, and the torn limbs of the horse lay scattered round, whilst the man remained unhurt.

Blücher wished to refresh his tired men, for since we had left Chalons they had been fighting daily. I was not present in those engagements; I heard now and then the noise of the battle near us, as at Mery, but the distracted accounts which I collected confused my ideas, so that I can give no clear account of them.

As we remained in Laon without even the excitement of a contest, I fell into a state of mind and body which I can only attribute to complete exhaustion; I suffered from a nervous irritability which I tried to strive against in vain; the talking by day, and the snoring by night, were insupportable, and such a weariness of spirits overcame me, that even the object of the war had ceased to interest me. After I had dined one day with Gneisenau, I ventured to say a few words upon my state; I had made a principle of never obtruding myself or my wants and sufferings to notice during the winter, but I had now a fixed idea that nothing could cure me but some defined duty. I ventured, therefore, to entreat Gneisenau to employ me; "I feel," I said, "that my mind gets daily weaker; I fear to sink so low that I may never be fit for service of any kind again."

"My good friend," he answered, "the most active and most useful soldier must feel for weeks together that he is doing nothing: weariness is an inevitable element of the present war; I can understand, knowing your former life, that the trial is greater to you than to most; but take courage: Napoleon is at the last extremity; even some stupid blunder on our part cannot help him now; our campaign will soon be ended—in a few days, perhaps tomorrow, you may see that which will strengthen and restore you."

The kind sympathy of this great and good man will be ever dear in my remembrance; he convinced me that my state of mind was the consequence of illness, and so it proved; I was seized with fever and obliged to keep my room. Blücher in the meantime left Laon and proceeded to Fisme, while a few troops only remained in Laon. It was impossible for me to march, I therefore remained some days in perfect quiet with my kind host and his family. I declined all medicine, being certain that my complaint was only utter prostration of strength from continual fatigue and exhaustion.

I slept soundly the greater part of every day. My host furnished me with a few books, neither very interesting nor instructive it is true, but they soothed and tranquillized my spirits like a gentle tonic. I strolled out sometimes; I had scarcely seen the inhabitants before, and now, as they again filled the handsome streets, and traces of social life peeped forth, I felt refreshed with the remembrance of times of peace, and was soon convalescent.

Accompanied by my servant and my two militiamen, I rode towards Rheims; we met many parties of Russians and Prussians on the road, and I proceeded with my small escort as safely as if in a friendly country. As we passed by Sillery the Russians were in the act of pillaging the celebrated cellars of Madame de Genlis, and I was glad to taste the delicious wine of that much-esteemed authoress; I am compelled to say that I derived more satisfaction from her wine than from her books.

While I was sleeping away my time in Laon, Saint Priest had taken Rheims: Blücher had passed a few days there and had again left it. I remained for a few days there in the house of a wine-merchant, who treated us well; a room where I could rest quietly alone, and the opportunity of cleansing and repairing in some degree my tattered wardrobe, helped to restore me to my usual health; I was again all cheerfulness and eager for the war. I joined the head-quarters near La Fere-Champenoise, and there was present at a scene which I shall never forget.

It was nearly noon when, headed by General Pacthod, we attacked a large squadron. They were drawn up in a square before a morass and waited our onset. A few charges of our cavalry were repulsed, some guns were brought and the square was assailed with a heavy discharge of grape-shot: the brave firmness with which the enemy stood it was wonderful; at length a large body of troops appeared on some considerable heights to the westward; it was a corps of the main army. Our King and the Emperor Alexander were there. The enemy's square were quite surrounded, and could not retire, as they intended, upon the marsh behind them; not only was the grape-shot continued, but a general fire from the troops was opened upon them.

I was riding by General Gneisenau: he approached the enemy, threw back his cloak, and stood before the hostile line in his splendid uniform and decorations; he addressed them, showed how hopeless their position was, and conjured them not to compel us to commit a useless slaughter; they had but to look round to see how they were hemmed in on every side; their heroism had already won our admiration, and they might surrender with untainted honour. While he spoke our guns had all been silent. The square closed more firmly up; a few shots from them were the only answer. Herr von Thiele, now minister of state, was then sent as the King's adjutant, to make a remonstrance. The conduct of the brave men had amazed us all and excited the deepest interest. Our troops continued to arrive from every side of the wide plain, and the square was pressed on closer every minute; the spectacle in the clear evening light became tragically grand.

The enemy's commander refused to listen to the King's adjutant. The latter was seized, and placed in the midst of the square, which stood more resolute than ever; and he had to remain there, exposed to the fire from his friends. The square was now attacked on every side. Some cannon-balls from our main body fell in the midst of us. I can declare that I never thought of danger. I was wholly absorbed in the amazing sight of a mass of men standing to defend themselves to the last from their plainly inevitable doom. We made a furious charge of cavalry. Gneisenau led it, and I followed him. The broken mass gave way, and I found myself at his side in the middle of the square. For one minute the enemy's fire ceased.

At that moment a lady rushed up to us: she seemed to be the wife of one of the superior officers. The broken ranks were now trying to form again, while a few shots only fell about us. Compared with the former simultaneous defence of the indomitable troops, these few scattered shots seemed like sobs of the subsiding wind after a hurricane: we scarcely heeded them. The lady approached the general, craving protection. He seemed struck with compassion, and gave her over to my care. It was a serious duty, and a new one. I got off my horse, and had moved with her only a few steps, in the hope of withdrawing her to a place of safety, when one of the staff rode up, and asked what I meant to do.

Confessing my uncertainty as to which way to turn, he claimed the office of protector, and I gladly surrendered it, hoping he might manage better for her than I could. In the short time I was with her she seemed more excited than terrified by the scene, and showed more manly firmness than womanly fear; but when the remembrance of the fate of those who were dear to her came over her, her grief broke out; and she wrung her hands, and seemed to forget all idea of danger for herself. The officer to whom I resigned her took her away, and I never heard again of her and her misfortunes.

Some minutes passed while I was thus engaged; when I returned the scene was completely changed. Here and there a few of the enemy still discharged their weapons in despair; but the square had disappeared; the prisoners were conveyed away, and the field was covered with the dead and dying.

A frightful barter followed on the scene of carnage. Russian lancers jumped off their horses, stuck their lances with the small flags into the ground to fasten their horses, and began to strip the bodies. Even the dying were not spared: those, however, to whom relief might yet be given were kindly treated and removed. While some were thus plundering, others were offering the articles for sale: boots, clothes, watches, &c., were bought as bargains by those who wanted them. A fine horse was offered to me for a few dollars. I could not make up my mind to buy, but many called me foolish for not having done so.

I hastened towards the general, who was much elated. The advantage we had won was important. "Now, Steffens," he cried, "what has become of your *ennui?*"

"If you keep me thus employed," I said, "I shall fear no return." Many years after I saw accidentally, in a list of those who had gained the Iron Cross, that I had received that honour on the occasion just described.

This most interesting affair closed the winter campaign. We advanced, through towns and villages which were well known to us, to La Ferté-sur-Jouarre. We passed the eventful forest of Etoges, and moved quietly and pleasantly one fine morning through the streets of Champaubert, and over the hills which on the day of doubt and danger had hidden Montmirail from sight. In two days we reached Meaux, and there the junction of the great army with the Silesians took place.

The press and confusion in the town of Meaux was frightful. From early dawn till late at night the endless stream was like the compressed waters of a swollen flood hurrying through a narrow passage between walls of rock: it poured on continually along the streets from one end of the town to the other. All the inhabitants were shut up in their houses; we did not venture into the throng. Cannon and ammunition-waggons, cavalry and foot, were pressed together close up to the walls of the houses. We were in a house in a rather long street, and, although the sight beneath us was truly wonderful, it became wearisome at last. A young officer thought it his duty to point out to the Field-Marshal that a man was stationed at an open window, taking note of the numbers of the troops. Blücher laughed out loud. "Let him be quiet; if he can keep count, and not lose his patience, so much the better; I hope he will reach Paris before we do, and take his news there."

CHAPTER 14

Armistice
1814

We stood before Paris; the position of the forces was unknown to me; the hills of Pantin and Montmartre hid the city entirely from us; Blücher's corps were fighting in the distance; the two hills were before us, the town of St. Denis just behind. Our headquarters were assembled on a wide extended plain; but of the battle, and the state of Paris, I knew nothing. The day before I had made a long march, in a state of great excitement. I had passed the night without sleep; and as we stood there on the field, hour after hour, far from the troops, and unable to gain any clear intelligence, our impatience rose to a painful pitch; thrown back upon myself, I was at last overcome with a most provoking lethargy; we had left our horses farther back; I wrapped myself in my cloak and fell into a sound sleep.

When I awoke I found myself alone, I could not see a soul over the whole wide plain, and I saw cannon-balls thickly strewed all round me, which had ploughed up the earth. I knew not which way to turn, and it was long before I found headquarters; they had moved to the right, closer to Montmartre. I then learnt that the generals had changed their posts because the enemy had observed them, and the cannonade had been hot upon the place. There had been some firing there earlier, and it must have been resumed while I slept; it had not waked me, and I had stood a good chance of a tranquil passage to another world.

News of the advance of our army increased, and reports of the movements in Paris, of early attempts to defend the city, and subsequent abandonment of the intention, became stronger. The French forces still sought to maintain Montmartre. It was again a lovely spring evening. Gneisenau, surrounded by some officers, stood on the plain, when a French officer approached—it was Bourgoing, son of the author, and he brought news of the armistice. Whilst he delivered his message a shell fell into an ammunition-waggon close by us; the waggon-driver cut the harness instantly, and galloped away, Bourgoing looked round very umcomfortably, but Gneisenau only moved slowly away.

A tremendous explosion took place, the fragments flew in great curves above our heads, and Gneisenau quietly continued his speech; he gave me orders to carry the news of the concluded armistice to the Russian troops, who were still fighting at Montmartre.

I joined the advanced guard on the hill, which was thickly covered with bushes; they were still engaged, and it was some time before the dispersed riflemen could be recalled; the enemy withdrew at the same time, and a strange stillness succeeded. I mounted the hill; the Russians entered the city, and Gneisenau appeared a few minutes later.

Through the geognostic researches of Cuvier and Brongniart, I thought I was familiar with the locality of the hill of Montmartre and the environs, and I offered myself as guide to the general; we were both naturally burning with desire to behold the city of Paris, lying at our feet. I led him and his followers through a street, which, however, was closed up at the end with houses. "Paris must be there, that is quite certain," said I, as Gneisenau turned to me with a smile, and an inquiring "Well?" A great door stood just before us to the left; we passed through it, and found ourselves in a churchyard bounded by a low wall. The great city which we had conquered lay before us in the glowing evening light, and I stood by Gneisenau.

I folded my hands; a prayer breathed silently from my lips; it was the greatest, the holiest moment that I ever lived. Every incident of the eventful time since my secret and distant correspondence with Gneisenau first began in Halle—our concealed meetings in Breslau— the outbreak of the war—the whole campaign, with its confused events and brilliant victories, all swept before my memory; and now Paris, and with her the giant who had shaken Europe, lay powerless at our feet. I saw the mighty city which for centuries had constrained and influenced the mind of Europe—the city which, till now, could call herself the greatest, the metropolis of civilization.

My thoughts flew farther, and again they turned within. They reverted to the time when, as I greeted with enthusiasm the German soil, I had first perceived the coming storm. I remembered how I had traced it as it slowly rose, and how it at last broke over us; and now it had cleared away, and a cloudless heaven once more shone above us. The clear fine evening reflected the bright dream which entranced me.

I was quartered in Montmartre in the same house with General Gneisenau, and towards noon he came into my room with his look of kind perplexity. I saw plainly that he had something to tell me which he feared might be unpleasant. He spoke at first of various subjects— of scenes of the campaign—of acknowledgment of the small services which I had rendered—and plainly tried to put me in good spirits. At last the unwelcome message must be told:—"Dear Steffens," he said, "at twelve o'clock today the Emperor and the King of Prussia are to make their triumphal entry into Paris: those troops which have suffered least in the campaign are to attend; the officers will appear in full uniform.

I interrupted him quickly, laughing; it was the last thing I should desire to make one of such a show—my appointments were not fit for a parade. I assured him that to be excluded would be far from an annoyance; my intention was to glide privately about Paris, and not to be a blot in the splendid spectacle. Some of my companions were as little producible as myself; we should take our chance to find our way, and doubtless we should find some German friends who would direct us. Gneisenau was satisfied.

We waited till the generals and officers, in their best array together with the troops, had left the suburb. We then rode by a rough and steep road down into the Faubourg Montmartre. The streets were empty; we only saw a few persons who were hastening forward, and we thought it wise to follow the direction which they took. We thus reached the Boulevard at the moment when the Emperor and King were passing in slow and magnificent procession along the handsome row of buildings. Immense crowds thronged the streets which led to the Boulevard; but the military had taken care to preserve the line of procession perfectly free for the conquerors.

Every window was filled with spectators shouting forth acclamations, the ladies in their gayest dresses; white handkerchiefs waved from the windows, and a shower of white lilies fell from every story upon the victorious enemy. Every well-dressed man in the streets wore a white cockade. One would have taken the scene for the triumphant entrance of a French army which had annihilated a dangerous and detested foe. Yet at that very moment the hero who had subdued the whole continent of Europe, and who had made France the ruler of the nations, surrounded by but a few faithful troops, and deserted by his people, was sinking to destruction.

I confess that in that moment the Parisians were contemptible in my sight. Napoleon had not been so received in Germany. Berlin had seen him enter with a silent but bitter rage. As we hastened silently along the Boulevard, the unworthy spectacle damped the joy of our own triumph; I felt as if partaking the disgrace, and hid myself in one of the deserted streets.

We had no distinct idea of which way to proceed, and had reached the Theatre des Italiens when a young man addressed us: "Can you inform me whether Professor Steffens has accompanied the army to Paris?"

What a confirmation of my belief that I should not be long without discovering friends! He was a young doctor of medicine of Leipzig, who was studying comparative anatomy in Paris under Cuvier. He joined us, and assisted us to and at least temporary accommodation in an hotel.

I learned from my new acquaintance that Cuvier had told his classes that I had given up science and all my studies, and had embraced arms as a profession. He was the first person whom I visited. He received me politely, but seemed shy and afraid. At length he confessed the cause. It was believed that I was commissioned to carry off the collection in the *Jardin des Plantes*. I assured him that such an act of violence would be contrary both to German feelings, and to their enlightened estimation of the use and meaning of such treasures; that the collection owed its value chiefly to the presence of the man who had arranged and who could illustrate it.

All the collections of works of art were thrown open to the conquerors. I hastened to the Louvre; there I found evidence of the same apprehensions which had seized Cuvier, but which seemed to have been quieted by the assurances of the two sovereigns. When I entered, the Laocoon, the Apollo, and the Venus stood out in their places in the Great Hall, but were entirely enclosed in brickwork; they were just being opened out again, the heads of the Laocoon peeped forth from their covering, and the proud face of the Apollo looked out above the wall. The Venus was half uncovered, and I saw her rise, not from the waves, but from the bricks.

Our relations with the French people still seemed to me most unsatisfactory and dubious. I must confess that the results of our great struggle brought both to me and many others a feeling of disappointment. I had expected and desired a gentle and respectful treatment of the conquered enemy in the midst of their splendid capital; especially whilst surrounded by our army, my feelings would have advocated the greatest possible forbearance; but when I saw that forbearance changed into adulation, when I saw our sovereigns take the attitude of leaders of barbarians, while they looked on Paris as the metropolis of the world, I thought of Attila before Rome, and my sorrow and vexation knew no bounds. I saw how our strength was injured in its holiest principle, how it was wasted and degraded into a servile subjection; could the Parisians when they greeted our arrival have foreseen this, they might indeed have shouted out for joy; how far off was yet our genuine victory!

It is almost impossible to give a clear account of those few agitated days, into which so many discrepancies were crowded; on the second day I removed with my friend Häckel to another hotel. In order to authorize my stay in Paris, I was placed on the staff of the *commandant*, it being, however, understood that no claims would be made upon my time. The small service which was attached to the appointment was performed by deputy. I was quartered in the palace of one of the emigrant nobles, at the corner of the Rue de Beaune and of the Quai du Pont Royal, just opposite the Louvre; my windows looked upon the Quai.

One great inconvenience which was suffered in Paris was an extraordinary want of money, and it was felt by persons of the highest rank, even by the King himself. We were the more perplexed because, with the exception of free quarters, we lived in all other respects as travellers, and our expenses were enormous. I went to the superintendent-general to complain of my destitution, but was not listened to. I left him with very angry feelings, and as I met at that moment two officers whom I knew, together with another who was a stranger, I mentioned my fruitless application, and vented my annoyance by some hasty and severe expressions which were not customary with me, and which I was in the habit of blaming when I heard them used by others to the commissariat; in fact, throughout the campaign that department had fulfilled their duties admirably under most difficult circumstances.

My expressions would have been quite harmless if spoken only before friends, but, unluckily, I was deficient in the organ of discriminating uniforms; the third officer was a commissary. He hastened to complain of my conduct to his chief, from whom I received a most severe letter, informing me that he should lay a complaint before the field-marshal. I made a proper apology, but he reported me, and my annoyance was extreme; on the second day, however, I received an invitation from Blücher to breakfast with him; several officers were present, and he approached me with a cheerful countenance: "Steffens," he said, "there is a charge laid against you; you ought to know one must not d—— the d—— in his presence."

I related my unhappy incapability of remembering uniforms; the party all laughed: oysters and champagne were brought, and partaken of in high good humour: thus my military career concluded with a charge and a punishment which I found extremely bearable.

An evening which I passed at the Grand Opera within a few days of our arrival is worth describing. I had succeeded in getting a place immediately before the orchestra; it was the first time I had seen a French theatre, and my admiration was great, as I leaned against the barrier which divided the orchestra from the pit, and watched the filling of the house. Some slight agitation, which began, first among a few, but which gradually spread to be more general, convinced me that other entertainment was in preparation besides the performance of the opera.

The opposite parties had in fact determined that evening on a national demonstration. Spontini sat in the orchestra just before me, and I perceived, to my surprise, that the music of two operas lay before him; neither was as yet set up, so I was able to read the titles; one was the *Triumph of Trajan*, the other Spontini's *Vestal*. I guessed that the choice between these was to decide the demonstration; and so it proved.

The uproar began: part of the audience clamoured for the *Triumph of Trajan*, the rest for the *Vestal*. As I afterwards learnt, the first had been proposed by the opera-corps, who were in the Napoleon interest: the public seemed divided—the two opinions balanced and wavered, and the supporters of each were deafening in their exertions. In Tieck's *Puss in Boots* an audience is represented as falling into a rage with the performance; a peace-maker appeared, and ordered the air from the Zauberflöte to be sung, '*In diesen heiligen Hallen kennt man die Rache nicht*'—'Rage is not known within these holy halls;' and the violence of anger was charmed into enthusiastic applause.

An imitation of this scene was attempted in Paris; the song, '*Vive Henri Quatre*,' was played, many voices joined, and all applauded; the public seemed pacified, the curtain rose, and the chorus of Vestals appeared; a tremendous outcry, however, stopped the performance; the curtain fell once more and the contest began again more furiously than ever: men now appeared in the royal box, ladders were brought in, and the imperial eagle which hung in front was displaced in the midst of a stormy mixture of hisses, groans, and applause: more than another hour elapsed, while each party shouted, and the song was reattempted at intervals with decreasing power, to still the raging tempest; at last, during a momentary pause, a voice cried out for a deputation to be sent to the Emperor Alexander, to represent to him that the public would be satisfied to submit to his decision.

The strife continually increased in fierceness and intensity till the messengers who had been sent to the Emperor returned; as they leaned over the front boxes, perfect stillness succeeded to the noise. The Emperor sent word that whichever piece it might suit the pleasure of the honoured public to choose would be approved by him. Since the contending parties seemed by this answer to receive a sanction for their strife, they renewed it with more vigour than before; there were times when I apprehended personal violence, and that our evening would conclude with a real tragedy.

As the struggle became more serious a fresh message was sent to the Emperor, and an answer was brought back choosing the Vestal: :he public instantly submitted to the imperial decision, and about midnight all settled themselves down to listen, with as much quiet attention as if it were the usual hour, and they had all just left their domestic occupations to enjoy the evening with their families; even between the acts all was orderly as usual, and, when a long ballet had succeeded, the large assembly separated without any further demonstration of feeling.

Paris presented a singular spectacle: everybody who had money and leisure poured into it from every quarter of Europe; and whilst the conquerors were treating the inhabitants with singular consideration, riches flowed in upon them from all sides. The number of English was very great.

As I entered Very's one morning I found Blücher there with two of his adjutants; he was perfectly recovered and in high spirits, and asked me many questions about the newly broken out Norwegian war. Blücher was by no means a partisan of Bernadotte, his sympathy was all for Norway: he spoke with great animation, and treated me kindly and confidentially. When I was obliged to go I left Blücher still there: the room was filled with French and English, who had listened with curiosity to our conversation, though they could not understand a word.

As I made my way out two Englishmen approached me respect-fully: they concluded by my intercourse with Blücher that I must be in some important station, and asked timidly if that were really the great hero?—a great number of English had come to Paris on pur-pose to look at him. When I answered in the affirmative they turned towards the table where he sat, and were lost in contemplation; an ah! of admiration was all that I heard from them; they folded their hands, and I never saw such a picture ,of silent veneration; even I came in for a share of their admiration.

Then I imagined myself transported into foreign lands at a great distance from France. I thought to myself, would anyone believe me, unrenowned as I was, if I were to relate that I had seen the whole war by the side of Blücher? would they not regard it as an inconceivable invention? Round his head was bound every victorious laurel which had been plucked from Napoleon's dreaded brow; and must not some faint ray of honour glance on me, when I should oblige them to be-lieve that such a happiness had been my portion?

When the Emperor Napoleon abdicated and was sent to Elba, I petitioned the King to grant me my release from military service; and as soon as the first credible reports of Napoleon's dethronement be-came general, I sent for a tailor to make my outer man myself again. I can hardly describe my sense of freedom when I put off my uni-form; the long-worn dress was hateful to me, however I may have been honoured in the right to wear it; all my linen was sent to take a swimming-bath in the Seine, and I felt as if I were born again.

My petition received the following answer:—

Since it appears to me that you will now more effectually serve the State by returning to your scientific appointment than by continuing longer in your present position in the army, I grant your petition to be released from military service, and together with this discharge I join my assurance that I acknowledge with thanks the patriotic self-sacrifice with which you laudably pre-ceded your fellow-citizens in the hour of danger.

Frederick Wilhelm.

H. Q., Paris, May 5th, 1814.

Blücher with some of his officers was preparing to go to London, and he proposed to me to accompany him. I was truly grieved to be obliged to decline this most kind offer. My circumstances would not permit the great expense which I must have incurred to have appeared in the midst of military splendour in that luxurious city. I therefore parted from Blücher, Gneisenau, and all the kind friends who surrounded them. As I took leave of them, the events which I had seen in the company of those great men swept before my thoughts in all their historical importance, and I was deeply affected.

At my request the minister of state had supplied me with a courier passport and a sum of money to defray my journey. I might have returned with the army, but my earnest longing to join my family, and resume my quiet academic duties, increased daily, and prompted me to determine on an immediate departure. I must not omit to record my last dilemma. My passport had been made out to "The Second-Lieutenant and Professor Dr. Steffens." I protested against the arrangement of these titles. I presented that I must stand by my real profession, and not that which I had only provisionally followed.

I asked my kind friend who made out the passport whether, supposing the title of Second-Lieutenant to be superior, I could in future designate myself Mr. Second-Lieutenant without disparaging my academic face. After much discussion on the point, I made a proposal which would avoid the question of the precedence of my two characters—that instead of Mr. Second-Lieutenant and Professor, &c. &c., I should be styled Second-Lieutenant Mr. Professor, &c. &c. This was adopted, and the difficulty happily alleviated.

LEONAUR

ALSO FROM LEONAUR
AVAILABLE IN SOFTCOVER OR HARDCOVER WITH DUST JACKET

FARAWAY CAMPAIGN *by F. James*—Experiences of an Indian Army Cavalry Officer in Persia & Russia During the Great War.

REVOLT IN THE DESERT *by T. E. Lawrence*—An account of the experiences of one remarkable British officer's war from his own perspective.

MACHINE-GUN SQUADRON *by A. M. G.*—The 20th Machine Gunners from British Yeomanry Regiments in the Middle East Campaign of the First World War.

A GUNNER'S CRUSADE *by Antony Bluett*—The Campaign in the Desert, Palestine & Syria as Experienced by the Honourable Artillery Company During the Great War .

DESPATCH RIDER *by W. H. L. Watson*—The Experiences of a British Army Motorcycle Despatch Rider During the Opening Battles of the Great War in Europe.

TIGERS ALONG THE TIGRIS *by E. J. Thompson*—The Leicestershire Regiment in Mesopotamia During the First World War.

HEARTS & DRAGONS *by Charles R. M. F. Crutwell*—The 4th Royal Berkshire Regiment in France and Italy During the Great War, 1914-1918.

INFANTRY BRIGADE: 1914 *by John Ward*—The Diary of a Commander of the 15th Infantry Brigade, 5th Division, British Army, During the Retreat from Mons.

DOING OUR 'BIT' *by Ian Hay*—Two Classic Accounts of the Men of Kitchener's 'New Army' During the Great War including *The First 100,000* & *All In It*.

AN EYE IN THE STORM *by Arthur Ruhl*—An American War Correspondent's Experiences of the First World War from the Western Front to Gallipoli-and Beyond.

STAND & FALL *by Joe Cassells*—With the Middlesex Regiment Against the Bolsheviks 1918-19.

RIFLEMAN MACGILL'S WAR *by Patrick MacGill*—A Soldier of the London Irish During the Great War in Europe including *The Amateur Army*, *The Red Horizon* & *The Great Push*.

WITH THE GUNS *by C. A. Rose & Hugh Dalton*—Two First Hand Accounts of British Gunners at War in Europe During World War 1- Three Years in France with the Guns and With the British Guns in Italy.

THE BUSH WAR DOCTOR *by Robert V. Dolbey*—The Experiences of a British Army Doctor During the East African Campaign of the First World War.

LEONAUR

ALSO FROM LEONAUR
AVAILABLE IN SOFTCOVER OR HARDCOVER WITH DUST JACKET

THE 9TH—THE KING'S (LIVERPOOL REGIMENT) IN THE GREAT WAR 1914 - 1918 *by Enos H. G. Roberts*—Mersey to mud—war and Liverpool men.

THE GAMBARDIER *by Mark Severn*—The experiences of a battery of Heavy artillery on the Western Front during the First World War.

FROM MESSINES TO THIRD YPRES *by Thomas Floyd*—A personal account of the First World War on the Western front by a 2/5th Lancashire Fusilier.

THE IRISH GUARDS IN THE GREAT WAR - VOLUME 1 *by Rudyard Kipling*—Edited and Compiled from Their Diaries and Papers—The First Battalion.

THE IRISH GUARDS IN THE GREAT WAR - VOLUME 1 *by Rudyard Kipling*—Edited and Compiled from Their Diaries and Papers—The Second Battalion.

ARMOURED CARS IN EDEN *by K. Roosevelt*—An American President's son serving in Rolls Royce armoured cars with the British in Mesopatamia & with the American Artillery in France during the First World War.

CHASSEUR OF 1914 *by Marcel Dupont*—Experiences of the twilight of the French Light Cavalry by a young officer during the early battles of the great war in Europe.

TROOP HORSE & TRENCH *by R.A. Lloyd*—The experiences of a British Lifeguardsman of the household cavalry fighting on the western front during the First World War 1914-18.

THE EAST AFRICAN MOUNTED RIFLES *by C.J. Wilson*—Experiences of the campaign in the East African bush during the First World War.

THE LONG PATROL *by George Berrie*—A Novel of Light Horsemen from Gallipoli to the Palestine campaign of the First World War.

THE FIGHTING CAMELIERS *by Frank Reid*—The exploits of the Imperial Camel Corps in the desert and Palestine campaigns of the First World War.

STEEL CHARIOTS IN THE DESERT *by S. C. Rolls*—The first world war experiences of a Rolls Royce armoured car driver with the Duke of Westminster in Libya and in Arabia with T.E. Lawrence.

WITH THE IMPERIAL CAMEL CORPS IN THE GREAT WAR *by Geoffrey Inchbald*—The story of a serving officer with the British 2nd battalion against the Senussi and during the Palestine campaign.

www.ingramcontent.com/pod-product-compliance
Lightning Source LLC
Chambersburg PA
CBHW021111090426
42738CB00006B/592